FAMOUS FROCKS

FAMOUS FROCKS

PATTERNS AND INSTRUCTIONS FOR RECREATING FABULOUS ICONIC DRESSES

Sara Alm & Hannah McDevitt

Illustrations by KERRIE HESS

CHRONICLE BOOKS
SAN FRANCISCO

Library of Congress Cataloging-in-Publication Data:
Alm, Sara.
Famous frocks : patterns and instructions for recreating fabulous iconic dresses /
Sara Alm & Hannah McDevitt.
p. cm.
ISBN 978-0-8118-7791-6 (hard cover)
1. Dressmaking–Patterns. 2. Actresses–Clothing.
3. Celebrities–Clothing. I. McDevitt, Hannah. II. Title.

TT520.A437 2011
646.4'04–dc22

2010044575

Manufactured in China
Designed by **Ayako Akazawa**

1 3 5 7 9 10 8 6 4 2

Chronicle Books
680 Second Street
San Francisco, California 94107
www.chroniclebooks.com

JELL-O® is a registered trademark of Kraft Foods.

INTRODUCTION

Bette Davis, Marilyn Monroe, Audrey Hepburn—these women are true fashion icons of their eras, and the dresses they wore still make us swoon. As trends come and go, the iconic styles of these stars hold strong and continue to influence the contemporary fashion we see on runways and in boutiques. While hints of Jackie, winks to Twiggy, and flashes of Madonna continue to show up in the clothes we wear today, there has yet to be a book that includes easy-to-sew dress patterns and shows, step by step, how to re-create these timeless looks on your own, in fabrics that speak to you.

In *Famous Frocks*, we have selected ten women from recent decades who we feel have the most inspiring and iconic looks, wearing dresses that stand the test of time and we absolutely adore. We chose famous dresses from the thirties up through the eighties, starting with the one and only Bette Davis and her glamorous bias-cut gowns and ending with a sexy "like a virgin" Madonna dress. In between, we also have Marilyn Monroe and her classic bombshell white halter; Jackie O's elegant crisp A-line; Audrey Hepburn's Little Black Dress; Twiggy and her minis; the fabulous Diana Ross; Farrah Fawcett's casual-chic wrap dress; and bohemian goddess Stevie Nicks. The fashion statements of these women can become yours as soon as your fabric is cut.

Until now the only way of achieving these kinds of looks was to scour thrift stores or hope to find a vintage sewing pattern—each feat frustrating in its own right. We know the feeling of finding the perfect Audrey dress in a thrift store, only to find out it is two sizes too small or has a big stain on the front. With vintage patterns, sizing and fit is always an issue—yes, we love the look of Rita Hayworth's dress, but we no longer wear the cone-shaped torpedo bras for which the pattern was cut. Now you can set your frustrations aside. As patternmakers and thrifters, we set out to conquer these frustrations and provide the patterns we have always wanted ourselves.

For each icon, there is a more direct interpretation of the dress as well as a variation that offers a creative new take on the look—like changing the neckline of a Jackie O. dress, or using stripes on Marilyn's classic white halter to create more geometric intrigue. There are patterns and instructions for twenty dresses in all (two for each icon), which means *lots* of opportunities for getting creative and having fun. So, if you've always envied Stevie Nicks's gypsy-cool look or Twiggy's playful little frocks, now is the time to dig in and start sewing that awesome dress you've admired but never see in stores. We hope that you'll interpret each dress to your own liking with the fabric selection, the accessories you choose, and the way you wear it for different occasions. Have fun and sew them up while listening to songs and watching movies from the era of each dress. Plus, you can see photos of the dresses we've made and submit your own finished dresses at www.chroniclebooks.com/famousfrocks. We think this book will not only teach you skills for fashion sewing but also bring out the Audrey Hepburn or Madonna in you, or both!

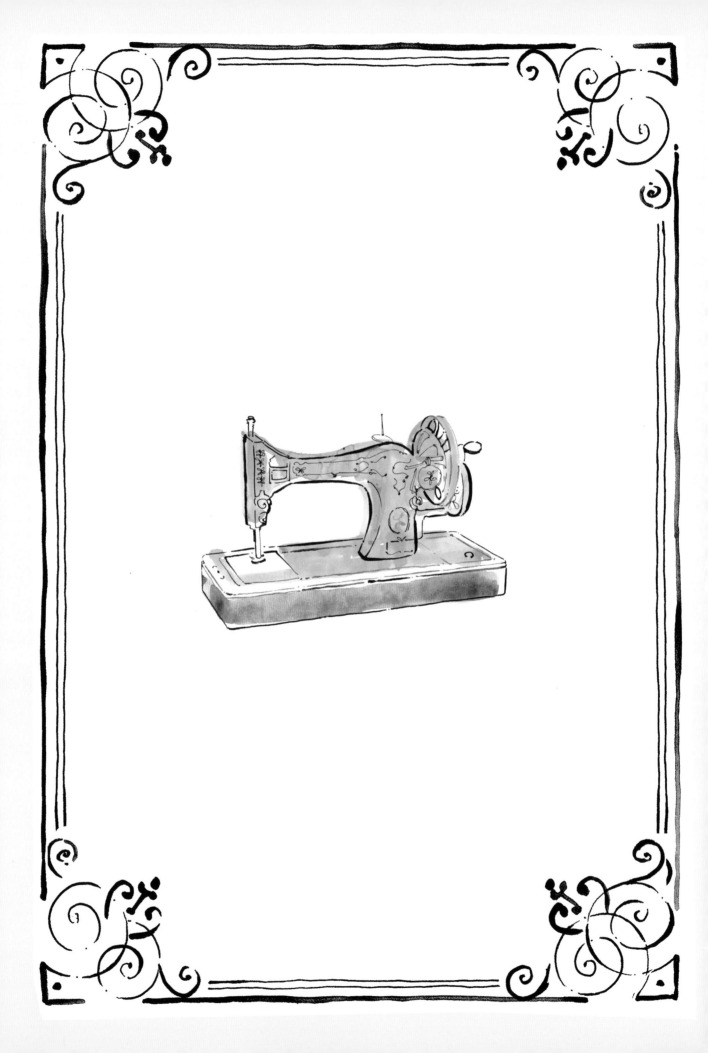

GENERAL INSTRUCTIONS

DETERMINE YOUR SIZE

All of the patterns are sized XS to L. Before you begin tracing off your pattern pieces it's important to take precise measurements. Please refer to chart below to determine which size will best suit your figure. If your measurements are between sizes, cut between lines on pattern pieces. If your bust, waist, or hip sizes differ from these sizes, blend lines between those size lines.

	XS	S	M	L
Bust	31 in 79 cm	33 in 84 cm	35 in 89 cm	37 in 94 cm
Waist (¼ in/6 mm above navel)	24½in 62 cm	26½ in 67 cm	28½ in 72 cm	30½ in 77 cm
Hip (8½ in/22 cm below navel)	34½ in 88 cm	36½ in 93 cm	38½ in 98 cm	40½ in 103 cm

READ ALL PATTERN INSTRUCTIONS

Read all of the instructions thoroughly before beginning your chosen project. Look over the cutting layout. Refer to the Terms, Techniques, and Tools section (pg. 137) for any instructions with which you may not be familiar.

TRACE OFF YOUR PATTERN

In this book the patterns are printed on both sides of the paper and some pattern pieces overlap others, so you will need to trace off your patterns. Lightweight butcher paper is best for tracing off your patterns and is widely available at many fabric and art supply stores. It's also handy to have a tracing wheel that will leave perforated markings on the butcher paper without distorting the original pattern. Use a ruler on the straight lines and be sure to transfer all pattern markings such as grainlines, notches, fold lines, and so on.

MAKE A MUSLIN

Before cutting into your lovely fabric, it's best to sew up a muslin. A muslin is traditionally made using muslin fabric (a lightweight woven cotton that's undyed and inexpensive). But if you are sewing one of the knit or bias dresses, it's important to select an inexpensive fabric with a similar stretch or drape ratio to the fashion fabric.

You do not need to worry about finishing off any seams. The purpose of sewing up a muslin is primarily to test the fit and make any alterations to the pattern before cutting out your fashion fabric.

SELECT YOUR FABRIC

Each chapter lists suggested fabrics that are ideal for each dress. Using a different fabric than what's listed may result in a different silhouette, drape, and fit. If you are using a fabric with nap or a directional print, purchase more fabric than listed in the instructions so that the print or nap of the fabric is facing in the same direction on all of the pattern pieces.

PREPARE YOUR FABRIC

It's important to prewash all fabrics before getting started. Prewashing will remove any excess dyes (so make sure to wash similar colors together) and possibly shrink the fabric a bit. After your fabric has been washed, it's important to press it. Make sure to set the temperature on your iron as is appropriate for the fabric. Gently move the iron along the fabric, working in small sections at a time, being careful not to distort the grain of the fabric. Dry-clean or hand wash any fabrics that cannot be machine washed.

CUT YOUR FABRIC

Each set of dress instructions contains a cutting layout indicating how the fabric is folded before the traced paper pattern pieces are laid on the fabric. Make sure all of the paper patterns' grainlines are perfectly parallel to the fabric's selvage edge, (the edge of the fabric that is bound and has not been cut). To achieve proper alignment, place a ruler perpendicular to the top of the grainline on the pattern and measure to the selvage, then measure again from the bottom of the grainline on the pattern, and adjust so that each measurement is equal. Pin or use weights to keep your pattern pieces in position as you cut your fabric out. After each pattern piece is cut, be sure to cut your notches, but no deeper than the triangular shapes themselves. Any patterns that have additional markings, such as darts, circle markers, fold lines, stitch lines, and buttonholes, should be transferred to the wrong side of your fabric.

A NOTE ON LENGTH

For the purposes of this book, the patterns are for short to mid-length dresses. To add length, adjust your paper pattern by measuring and marking 3 in/7.5 cm above the hem of the skirt on both sides of the pattern piece. Connect the two marks in a horizontal line. Cut along this line, and by placing extra paper behind the pattern, lengthen the pattern piece to your desired amount. Blend the lines of the side seam to create a smooth transition. Use the adjusted pattern to make your muslin to ensure proper length and fit. (This does not apply to the Stevie Nicks dresses, pages 116–123.) Please note that for the Bette Davis dress, you can choose to make this adjustment to the godets or not. If you keep the godets the original length, mark new circle markers on the skirt pattern pieces 14¼ in/36 cm above the adjusted hemline of the skirt pattern.

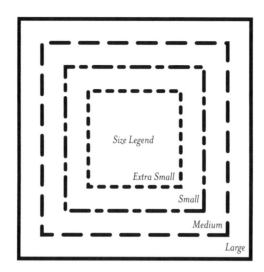

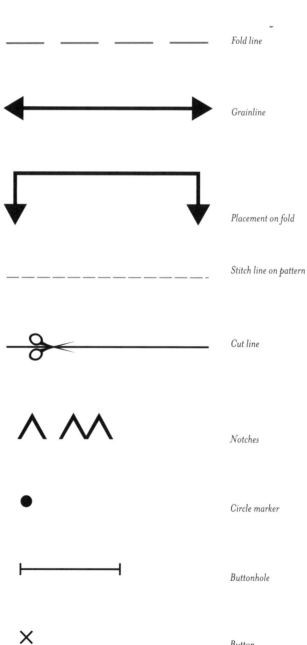

Fold line

Grainline

Placement on fold

Stitch line on pattern

Cut line

Notches

Circle marker

Buttonhole

Button

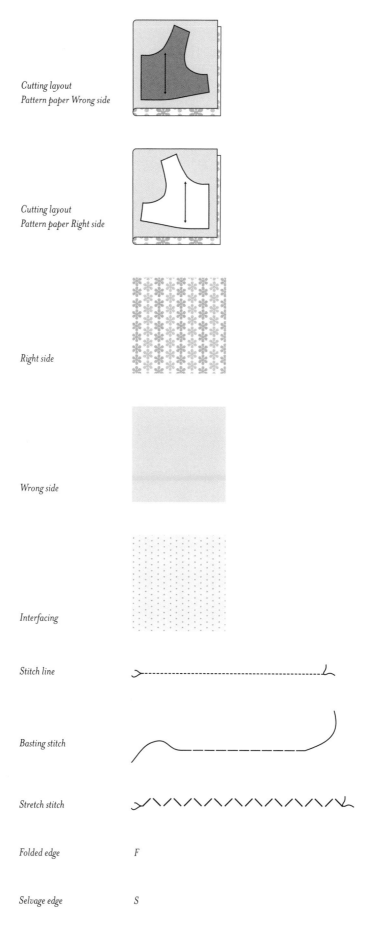

Cutting layout
Pattern paper Wrong side

Cutting layout
Pattern paper Right side

Right side

Wrong side

Interfacing

Stitch line

Basting stitch

Stretch stitch

Folded edge   F

Selvage edge   S

THE FROCKS

BETTE DAVIS

BETTE DAVIS

------ Sewing Level: Intermediate/Advanced ------

The Hollywood of the '30s and '40s teemed with slim blondes who sought sympathetic roles in pleasant films. Eschewing this ideal, Bette Davis, with her busty hourglass figure (considered "difficult" by Hollywood costume designers), took on unconventional roles, transforming herself into manipulators or killers. "What a fool I was to come to Hollywood," she said, "where they only understand platinum blondes and where legs are more important than talent." Indeed, Bette took the art of acting seriously, transforming herself physically to create an authentic look for each new character, even if the result was decidedly unattractive. She did not want to be a sex symbol and was such a fashion chameleon onscreen that her own style is difficult to pinpoint; yet she was named one of America's twelve best-dressed women by the New York–based Fashion Academy in the '30s, and she remains one of the ideals of old Hollywood glamour. Certainly, anyone who has seen Bette in the stunning evening dresses that she donned when not performing can understand why. She favored the fashionable bias-cut of the era, and she opted for low-back and shoulder-bearing pieces that highlighted her shoulders, adding drama with flutter sleeves, boleros, and capelets.

Both the icon dress and the variation are cut on the bias, with curved empire waistlines and princess seams. The cut of these dresses does not hug your body but gently skims over the curves, giving the dress an elegant sexiness.

To sew up a true Bette look, go for the icon dress with the fluttering flounce that starts at the shoulder seams and continues around to the deep center back seam. Be sure to insert the godets in between the skirt panels to play up the volume. In our interpretation of the icon dress, we chose a sheer contrast fabric for the flounce and godets. Choose the fabric combination that speaks to you.

The variation has less volume, though it shows a touch more skin. Without the flounce or the godets, this is a more modern and streamlined silver-screen dress. Make it to suit your tastes—to accentuate your shoulders and slim your hips, sew in just the flounce. Or keep the shoulders bare and insert the godets in the skirt to make it perfect for twirling.

{front}   {back}   {variation}

{variation}

SUGGESTED FABRICS

Silk Georgette, Crepe de Chine, Chiffon, Cotton Lawn

- - - YARDAGE - - -
3¾ yds/3.4 m (45 in/115 cm wide)

- - - NOTIONS - - -
20 in/50 cm zipper
Thread to match
Lightweight fusible knit interfacing: ½ yd/45 cm (44 in/112 cm wide) or 1 yard/90 cm (22 in/56 cm wide)

FOLLOW CUTTING LAYOUT FOR PATTERN PIECES

1 Center Front Bodice
2 Side Front Bodice
3 Center Back Bodice
4 Side Back Bodice
5 Center Front Skirt

6 Side Front Skirt
7 Center Back Skirt
8 Side Back Skirt
9 Godet (optional)

10 Shoulder Strap
11 Flounce (optional)
12 Front Neck Facing
13 Back Neck Facing

45 in/115 cm

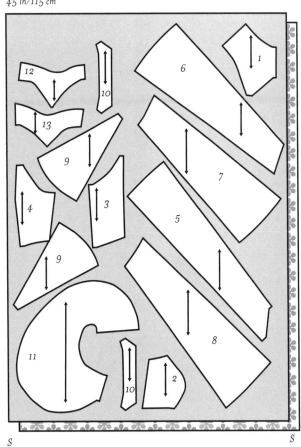

All seam allowances are ⅝ in/1.6 cm, unless otherwise indicated. Cutting should be done on two layers of unfolded fabric, **Right** sides together, lining up selvage edges. Make sure that if there is a nap or directional print both layers are facing in the same direction and your pattern pieces are laid out in accordance with the print or nap.

Tip: When working with fabrics with a lot of bias drape, make sure the fabric is squared up before pinning your pattern pieces to it. A self-healing mat and rotary cutter are ideal for keeping the fabric flat. If using scissors, make sure to keep the bottom of your scissors on the work surface as you cut.

1. Cut out all pattern pieces from fabric, following cutting layout. Cut out interfacing for pieces 10, 12, and 13.

2. Interface (refer to pg. 141) facings and straps.

3. Mark circle markers with transfer paper (refer to pg. 144), tailor's tacks (refer to pg. 144), or an awl (refer to pg. 144).

Tip: To keep bias cut fabric from stretching out, baste (refer to pg. 138) or stay stitch (refer to pg. 142) around the perimeter of all pattern pieces.

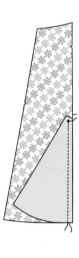

{fig. 1}

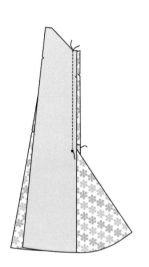

{fig. 2}

If you are not sewing godets, skip to the next section.

1. With **Right** sides together, place godet on the **Right** side panel of side front skirt, aligning circle markers. Starting with a short stitch length and increasing the stitch length setting to 2–3 as you go, sew from the circle marker to the hem of the skirt. {fig. 1}

2. With **Right** sides together, place the right center front skirt on top of side front skirt, aligning circle markers and notches. Pull the godet away from seam allowance. Using stitches from previous step to position needle at the beginning of the seam, start with a short stitch length and sew from the circle marker to the waistline of the skirt. {fig. 2}

3. Align the seam allowances of center front skirt and godet. Pull the side front skirt and excess godet away from seam allowance. Using stitches from previous steps to position needle at the beginning of the seam, start with a short stitch length and sew from the circle marker to the hemline of the skirt. {fig. 3}

4. Press all seams open. {fig. 4}

5. Repeat steps 1 through 4 for left side of skirt front.

6. Repeat steps 1 through 5 for center and side back skirt.

Tip: Pin, pin, pin! Fabrics cut on the bias have a tendency to shift as you sew. Use more pins to ensure that the two layers being sewn together maintain even seam length. Also hand baste the seams together before sewing for additional seam stability.

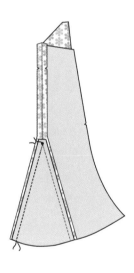

{fig. 3}

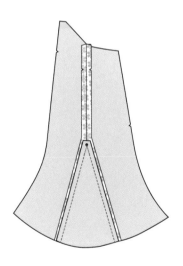

{fig. 4}

SKIRT WITHOUT GODETS

1. With **Right** sides together, sew center front skirt to side front skirt, aligning notches and circle markers. Press seam open. Repeat for second side.

2. With **Right** sides together, sew center back skirt to side back skirt, aligning notches and circle markers. Press seam open. Repeat for second side.

PREPARE THE BODICE AND STRAPS

1. With **Right** sides together, sew center back bodice to side back bodice. Press seam open. Repeat for second side. {*fig. 5*}

2. With **Right** sides together, sew strap to side back bodice along armhole, aligning notches. Press seam open, then toward strap. Repeat for second side.

3. With **Right** sides together, sew back neck facing to interfaced straps, aligning notches. Press seam open, then toward strap. Repeat for second side. {*fig. 6*}

{*fig. 5*}

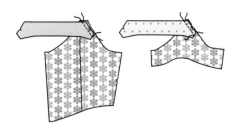

{*fig. 6*}

If not sewing the flounce, skip to the next section.

1. With **Right** sides facing, place flounce on dress back and straps, aligning neckline notch on flounce to seam line of strap/bodice join. Sew along neckline with a ¼-in/6-mm seam allowance. *{fig. 7}*

2. With **Right** sides together, place back neck/strap facing on top of flounce. Sew over stitches from previous step with a ¼-in/6-mm seam allowance, along neckline; the flounce will be sandwiched between the back bodice/strap and the back neck facing/strap pieces. *{fig. 8}*

3. Press seam allowances toward back neck/strap facing and understitch (refer to pg. 143).

4. Reposition back neck and strap facing on flounce so that **Right** sides are facing. Push flounce toward middle of armhole, to get it out of the way, as you sew a portion of each armhole seam.

5. Sew along armhole as far as you can sew (from front toward the back armhole) without catching the flounce. It may only be a small section that is sewn.

6. Sew along armhole as far as you can sew (from back toward the front armhole) without catching the flounce. Ideally, a small section of the strap will get sewn. *{fig. 9}*

7. Trim, clip (refer to pg. 139), and press seams open. Pull strap and flounce **Right** side out, so that the facing is forced to the **Wrong** side.

8. Press unsewn seam allowance on straps to **Wrong** side and hand sew closed.

9. Finish raw edge of flounce with either a rolled hem (refer to pg. 140) by hand, machine, or serger (refer to pg. 142), or leave edge raw and stay stitch (refer to pg. 142).

10. Baste flounce to strap front.

11. Repeat steps 1 through 10 for second side.

Tip: Insert a narrow wooden dowel or cardboard tube between facing and straps to aid in pressing strap seams open.

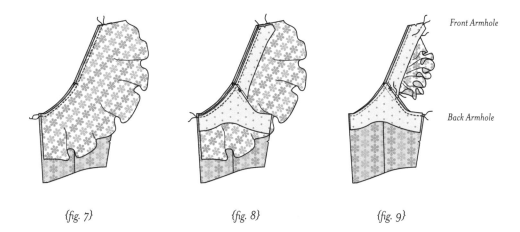

Front Armhole

Back Armhole

{fig. 7}　　　　{fig. 8}　　　　{fig. 9}

STRAP ONLY VARIATION

1. With **Right** sides together, place back neck/strap facing on back bodice. Sew along neckline with a ¼-in/6-mm seam allowance.

2. Press seam allowances toward back neck/strap facing and understitch (refer to pg. 143).

3. Reposition back neck/strap facing to back bodice so that **Right** sides are together. Sew along from front armhole toward the back armhole. Trim, clip, and press seam open. Turn **Right** side out, so that facing is forced to **Wrong** side, and press flat.

4. Repeat steps 1 through 3 for second side.

FRONT BODICE

1. Stay stitch side seams of center front bodice and clip seam allowance to release the curve.

2. With **Right** sides together, sew center front bodice to side front bodice. Press seam open. Repeat for second side. {fig. 10}

3. With **Right** sides together, place bodice front on flounce and/or strap, aligning notches; sew across unsewn edge of strap (and flounce). {fig. 11}

4. Turn bodice over and place front facing on strap (and flounce) with **Wrong** sides facing up. Sew from the center front seam, pivoting where neckline meets the strap, and continue to the side seam. {fig. 12}

5. Turn front facing to the **Wrong** side and press flat.

{fig. 10}

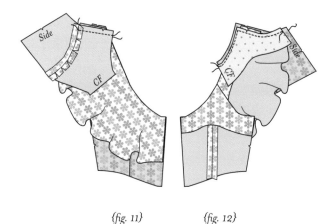

{fig. 11}   {fig. 12}

BODICE TO SKIRT

1. With **Right** sides together, sew bodice front to skirt front, aligning seam lines. Press seam open. Repeat for second side. {fig. 13}

2. With **Right** sides together, sew back bodice to back skirt, aligning seam lines. Press seam open. Repeat for second side.

3. With **Right** sides together, sew center front seam, folding the facing up, aligning notches and skirt, and facing seam lines. Press seam open, then press facing to **Wrong** side. {fig. 14}

4. With **Right** sides together, sew side front to side back, folding the facing up, aligning notches and skirt, and facing seam lines. Press seam open, then press facing to **Wrong** side. Repeat for second side.

5. Stitch in the ditch (refer to pg. 142) of the side seams, to tack down facings.

FINISHING

Tip: Let bias-cut dresses hang for a day or two before inserting the zipper or hemming, as the fabric will stretch over time. While wearing the dress, mark your desired hemline with a yardstick measuring up from the floor. Use tailor's chalk or pins to mark a cutting line or fold line.

1. Baste (refer to pg. 138) flounce to center back seam of bodice only, not including facing.

2. Insert invisible zipper (refer to pg. 140) between top edge and double notches on center back seam of skirt.

Tip: Baste invisible zipper between neckline and double notches on center back seam of skirt, then try on dress to check the position of the zipper; adjust if any ripples are forming.

3. Finish hem with a rolled hem (refer to pg. 140) by hand, machine, or serger, or leave edge raw and stay stitch (refer to pg. 142).

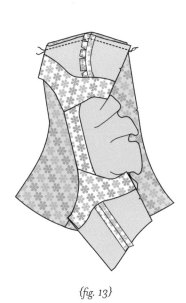

{fig. 13}

{fig. 14}

RITA HAYWORTH

RITA HAYWORTH

------ *Sewing Level: Beginner/Intermediate* ------

Rita Hayworth preferred baggy jeans and penny loafers to elaborate evening gowns, and she refused to pose nude, declaring that "all women have a certain elegance about them which is destroyed when they take off their clothes." And yet, Hayworth became the biggest sex symbol of her era and was nick-named the "Love Goddess" after her iconic role in *Gilda*. In perhaps the best example of how leaving a little to the imagination is often the sexiest style choice, Hayworth's *Life* magazine cover shot, in which she wore a full-length slip that revealed little more than her arms, became one of the most popular pin-up shots for service men in World War II. As the muse of Jean Louis, chief designer to the stars of Hollywood's "Golden Age," Hayworth was also a beauty icon for women of the time, playing characters whose costumes showcased how a modern, fashionable woman of the early '40s should dress. For the screen she chose glamorous, body-conscious gowns that showed off her long legs—at 5'6", Hayworth was tall for the time, posing a problem with some of her shorter dancing partners, notably Fred Astaire—and draped her frame in sultry gowns in luxurious materials such as silk, satin, and lace. The advent of Technicolor gave her red hair, crimson lips, and richly colored gowns even more va-va-voom vibrancy.

This dress is made for dancing. If you're in the mood for tango, sew up the icon dress with the longer sleeve and hem length. The center front and shoulder ruching is waist-slimming and makes your curves curvier. As if this isn't enough, there is also a bit of ruching just across the bum.

If your dancing plans are less ballroom and more nightclub, sew up the tunic length variation with an exposed zipper down the center front seam. The short sleeves gracefully drape around the upper arms. Both versions say va-va-voom in a way that would make Rita proud.

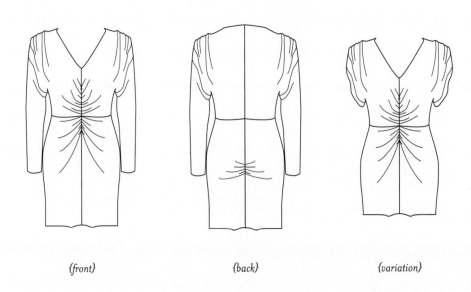

{front}   {back}   {variation}

{variation}

SUGGESTED FABRICS

Suitable for most light- to midweight 2- or 4-way stretch fabrics. Not suitable for rib knits.

- - - YARDAGE - - -
2¾ yds/2.5 m (60 in/150 cm wide)

- - - SHORT SLEEVE VARIATION - - -
1½ yds/1.4 m (60 in/150 cm wide)

- - - NOTIONS - - -
¼-in/6-mm wide elastic: ⅝ yd/57 cm
18 in/46 cm separating zipper
Thread to match

FOLLOW CUTTING LAYOUT FOR PATTERN PIECES

1 Bodice Front	4 Skirt Back	Elastic Guide for Center Back Seam
2 Bodice Back	5 Neck Facing	Elastic Guide for Center Front Seam
3 Skirt Front	Elastic Guide for Shoulder Seam	(not needed for Zipper Variation)

60 in/150 cm

Short Sleeve Variation
60 in/150 cm

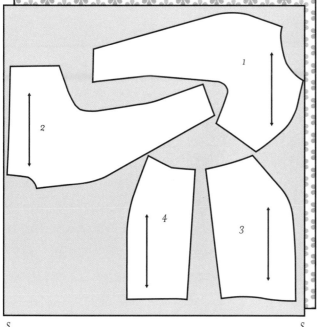

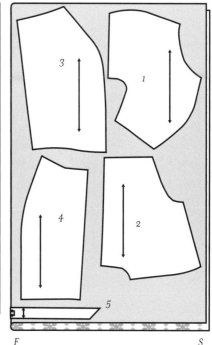

SEWING INSTRUCTIONS

All seam allowances are ⅝ in/1.6 cm, unless otherwise indicated. Use a stretch stitch (refer to pg. 143) on your machine for all seams, unless otherwise indicated.

Cut out all pattern pieces from fabric following cutting layout. Cut out the elastic using the elastic guide pattern pieces. For the long sleeve variation, cutting should be done on two layers of unfolded fabric, with **Right** sides together, lining up selvage edges. Make sure that if there is a nap or directional print that both layers are facing in the same direction and your pattern pieces are laid out in accordance with the print or nap.

BODICE FRONT

1. With **Right** sides together, sew bodice front to skirt front, aligning notches. Press seam open. Repeat for second side, making sure to have a right and left dress front. {fig. 1}

For Zipper Variation, skip the next three steps—go to Zipper variation.

2. Place dress fronts with **Right** sides together; using a ⅝-in/1.6-cm seam allowance, baste (refer to pg. 138) center front seam between notches aligning seam lines. {fig. 2}

3. Gather (refer to pg. 140) between notches until it is the length of the cut elastic for center front seam. {fig. 3}

4. Pin elastic over gathered seam, keeping the elastic relaxed, not stretched. Using a zigzag stitch, sew the entire length of the center front seam, from neckline to hemline; make sure to catch the elastic as you sew. Take your time! {fig. 4}

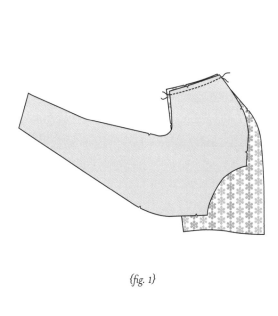

{fig. 1}

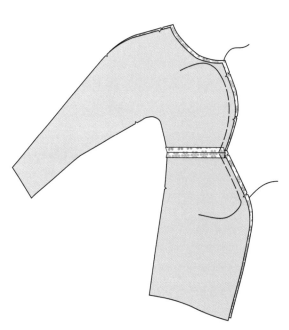

{fig. 2}

1. Using a ⅝-in/1.6-cm seam allowance, baste (refer to pg. 138) between notches on center front seam of one dress front. Repeat for second side.

2. Using the elastic guide for center front seam, gather (refer to pg. 140) each dress front to appropriate length for your size, making sure to gather evenly so that seam lines and notches will align. Note that you will not use elastic on the center front seam; use only the paper pattern piece as a guide.

3. With **Right** sides together, baste one dress front to zipper tape, leaving ⅝-in/1.6-cm for seam allowance at neckline and hem to finish seams. Repeat for second side. Close zipper and check for even gathering and aligned seam lines. Adjust as necessary.

4. Using a straight stitch, sew opened and separated zipper to dress front following basted stitches from step 3 as a guide. Press zipper tape to **Wrong** side. Repeat for second side.

Tip: When sewing a zipper in, move the zipper pull out of the way as you start your seam; then when you approach the zipper pull, lower the needle, lift up the presser foot, and pull the zipper pull back up and out of the way, lower your presser foot, and continue sewing.

5. Stitch in the ditch (refer to pg. 142) of the waistline seam to tack zipper tape and seam allowance to **Wrong** side. Repeat for second side.

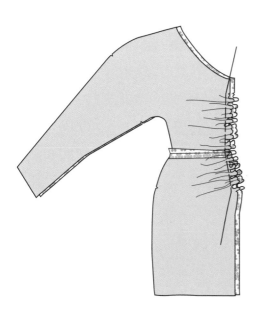

{fig. 3}

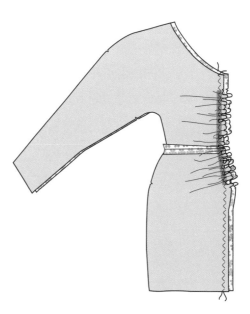

{fig. 4}

BODICE BACK

1. With **Right** sides together, sew bodice back to skirt back, aligning notches. Press seam open. Repeat for second side, making sure to have a right and left dress back. {*fig. 5*}

2. With **Right** sides together, using a ⅝-in/1.6-cm seam allowance, baste center back seam between notches.

3. Gather basted section until it is 3 in/7.5 cm in length, using the cut elastic for center back seam as a guide.

4. Pin elastic over gathered seam, keeping the elastic relaxed, not stretched. Using a zigzag stitch, sew the entire length of the center back seam from neckline to hemline, making sure to catch the elastic and align waist seam lines. {*fig. 6*}

SLEEVE

1. With **Right** sides together, place dress front on dress back. Using a ⅝-in/1.6-cm seam allowance, baste each shoulder seam between notches.

2. Gather each shoulder between notches until it is the length of the cut elastic for shoulder seam. {*fig. 7*}

3. Pin relaxed elastic over gathered seam. Using a zigzag stitch, sew shoulder seam from neckline to hemline of sleeve, catching the elastic as you sew. Repeat for second side. {*fig. 8*}

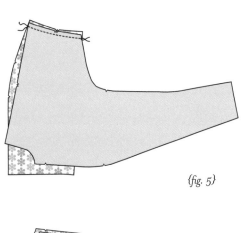

{*fig. 5*}

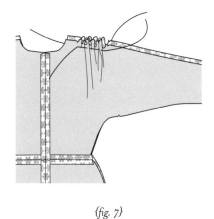

{*fig. 7*}

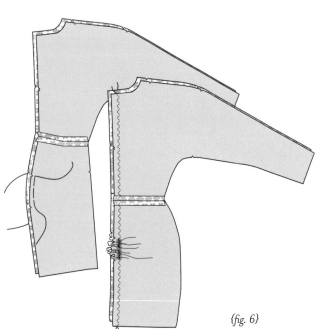

{*fig. 6*}

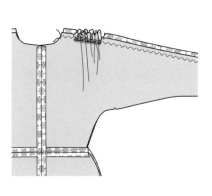

{*fig. 8*}

ATTACH THE FACING

Zipper Variation: Follow only steps 2, 4, and 5.

1. Sew center front seam of neck facing **Right** sides together. Press seam open. Skip this step for the zipper variation.

2. With **Right** sides together, stretch and pin neck facing to fit neckline of dress, aligning center front seams and notches to shoulder seams.

3. Sew around the neckline, starting and finishing at the center front seam. Clip at center front seam and press facing to **Wrong** side. Skip to step 5.

4. For Zipper Variation: Starting from the lower edge of the facing, sew up center front to neckline, pivot at neckline and continue around neck to center front on opposite side, pivot and sew down the center front to lower edge of facing. Trim corners and cut off any additional zipper tape that may be sticking out past the seam allowance. Turn **Right** side out, thereby forcing the facing to the **Wrong** side.

5. Topstitch (refer to pg. 143) with a twin needle (refer to pg. 143) ¼ in/6 mm from sewn edge around neckline. Cut away any excess neck facing that hangs below your topstitching.

Tip: When using a twin needle, always sew with the garment **Right** side facing up. Make sure to lower the thread tension on your machine.

SIDE SEAMS

1. With **Right** sides together, sew side seams, aligning notches and seam lines from sleeve hem to hemline of dress. Repeat for second side.

FINISHING

Press ⅝-in/1.6-cm hem allowance to **Wrong** side around hemlines of dress and sleeves. Topstitch with a twin needle.

Tip: Sew with sleeve inside out so as not to stretch it around the arm of your sewing machine as you sew. You will still be able to sew with the **Right** side of the sleeve facing up.

MARILYN MONROE

MARILYN MONROE

------ Sewing Level: Intermediate ------

Unlike Bette Davis, Marilyn Monroe embraced every aspect of being a femme fatale. She knew that her curvaceous frame—described as "Jell-O on springs" in *Some Like it Hot*—held the key to her fame, and she chose dresses that were cut for maximum sex appeal, accentuating her figure. Her fashion selections underscored her body awareness, and she opted for classic colors, such as champagne, black, brown, and—her favorite—white. By frequently having herself sewn into dresses, she ensured that her red carpet frocks were form-fitting and zipper free, needing no extra frills or embellishments. This white crepe halter dress, designed by William Travilla and worn in *The Seven Year Itch*, was voted the most iconic movie dress of all time and embodies the style sensibility of the original blonde bombshell.

You need not sew yourself into this dress; there is a zipper at center back. And trust us, it flatters more figures than just the hourglass. The fitted waist, 8-gore (panel) skirt says Marilyn all the way. The deep V-neck is, perhaps, slightly more conservative than what Marilyn would have preferred, but it's revealing nonetheless.

The icon dress features a halter back tie and the skirt gores are cut on the straight grainline of the fabric, making it a good choice for solid colors and all-over prints. The variation dress has straps that cross the back and button to the waistband. You can also add ruffles or piping to the center front bodice or in between every seam. The bias grainline of the skirt gores, cut out of a stripe or plaid fabric, play with geometry and create a diagonal or chevron pattern with the lines. For more bust support, interface or interline your bodice fabric with fusible fleece or flannel interlining.

{front}   {variation}

{variation}

SUGGESTED FABRICS

Cotton Sateen, Lightweight Linen, Silk Dupioni, Seersucker. For variation, use stripes/plaids.

- - - YARDAGE - - -
3⅜ yds/3.1 m (45 in/115 cm wide)
- - - Or - - -
2⅜ yds/2.2 m (60 in/150 cm wide)

For Bias Variation, allow extra yardage for lining up stripes or patterns:
3¾ yds/3.4 m (45 in/115 cm wide)
- - - Or - - -
2½ yds/2.3 m (60 in/150 cm wide)

½ yd/50 cm of contrast fabric to create ruffle trim

- - - NOTIONS - - -
12-in/30-cm zipper
Thread to match
⅛-in/3-mm piping: 3 yds/2.75 m
Two ¾-in/2-cm buttons
Lightweight fusible knit interfacing: ½ yd/50 cm (44 in/112 cm wide) or 1 yard/90 cm (22 in/55 cm wide). An additional
½ yd/50 cm (44 in/112 cm wide) is needed for bodice fronts with bust support and/or back cross straps.

FOLLOW CUTTING LAYOUT FOR PATTERN PIECES

1 Bodice Front   3 Skirt Gore   5 Waist Tie (optional)
2 Waistband   4 Neck Strap

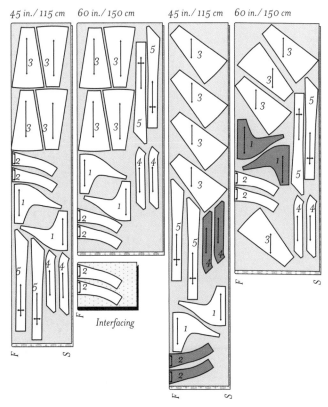

Bias Variation

45 in./115 cm   60 in./150 cm   45 in./115 cm   60 in./150 cm

Interfacing

SEWING INSTRUCTIONS

All seam allowances are ⅝ in/1.6 cm, unless otherwise indicated.

1. Cut out all pattern pieces from fabric, following cutting layout. Cut out interfacing for pieces 2 and, if desired, 1 and/or 4. For Bias Variation, be sure to align stripes appropriately to match.

Tip: To ensure proper pattern alignment for the bias variation, mark obvious stripes or prints onto pattern paper at seams where fabric design should line up. Use markings as guides to line up the fabric for the following skirt pieces. Ensure that the folded fabric is lined up as well.

2. Interface (refer to pg. 141) one waistband piece. For more bust support, fuse interfacing to bodice pieces or baste interlining to two bodices, a right and left. For cross back straps, interface two neck straps, a right and left.

3. For cross back strap variation, mark buttonhole placement on **Right** side of non-interfaced neck strap.

RUFFLE TRIM OPTION

1. Cut 2½-in/6.4-cm wide strips from self fabric or contrast fabric along the crosswise grain from selvage to selvage. Fold fabric **Wrong** sides together and sew 2 rows of basting stitches (refer to pg. 138) along raw edges of long side. Gather to desired effect on the bodice, straps and waistband.

When adding piping or ruffle trim, sandwich trim between bodice and waistband, and waistband and skirt with **Right** sides together, aligning raw edges, and sew as instructed below in the following sections: Prepare the Bodice step 1, Attach Bodice to Waistband step 1, and Attach Bodice to Skirt step 1.

NECK STRAPS

1. Place two straps **Right** sides together. Sew two long sides and the one angled side, pivoting at corners. Trim corners, press seams open and turn **Right** side out. Using a corner tool, gently push out any corners. Press strap flat and topstitch ¼ in/6 mm (refer to pg. 143) away from the three sewn edges. Repeat for second strap. *{fig. 1}*

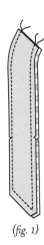

{fig. 1}

1. With **Right** sides together, sew two bodice fronts at center front neckline. Press seam open. With **Wrong** side facing up, press seam allowances toward self lining and understitch (refer to pg. 143); the understitched side will be the self lining. Repeat for second side, being sure to create a left and a right bodice. {*fig. 2*}

2. Fold bodice front pieces **Right** sides together. Sew bodice front to self lining along armhole curve. {*fig. 3*}

   If using piping or trim, sandwich trim along armhole curve with fabric **Right** sides together. Trim, clip (refer to pg. 139), and press seam open. Repeat for second side.

3. Insert neck straps between bodice front and bodice self lining with **Right** sides together and raw edges aligned. The interior curve of the neck strap is closest to the center front seam of the bodice. Sew along shoulder seam. Repeat for second side. {*fig. 4*}

4. Turn **Right** side out and press so that shoulder seams are flat.

5. Sew rows of basting stitches (refer to pg. 138) between notches on bodice. {*fig. 5*} Gather to fit between the notches on the interfaced waistband. {*fig. 6*} Repeat for second side.

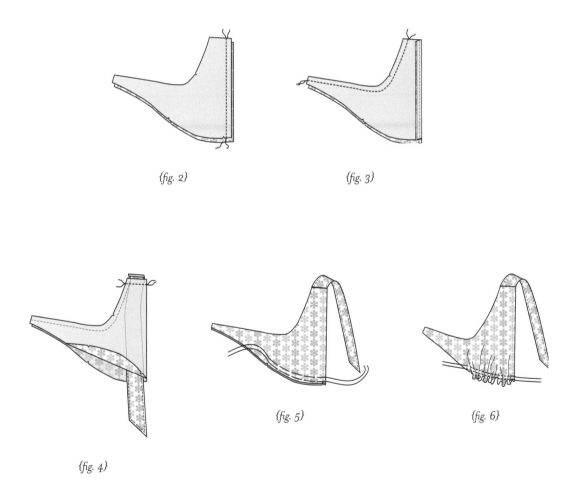

{*fig. 2*}

{*fig. 3*}

{*fig. 4*}

{*fig. 5*}

{*fig. 6*}

ATTACH BODICE TO WAISTBAND

1. With **Right** sides together, sew bodice fronts to interfaced waistband, aligning notches. Make sure bodice fronts match up with notches along the upper waistband.

2. Sew waistband facing to bodice fronts and outer waistband, with the **Right** side of the facing toward the **Wrong** side of the bodice fronts; bodice fronts should be sandwiched between interfaced waistband and waistband facing. Remove basting stitches on bodice. {fig. 7}

SKIRT

1. With **Right** sides together, sew one side seam of two gores from waistline to hem. Repeat for all eight gores, leaving one seam open for center back. Press seams open. {fig. 8}

Tip: For Bias Variations, pin skirt gores **Right** sides together very carefully, making sure to align stripes/patterns. Baste seams together (refer to pg. 138) to ensure proper alignment before sewing.

2. Stay stitch (refer to pg. 142) along upper edge of skirt within seam allowance.

ATTACH BODICE TO SKIRT

1. Sew interfaced waistband to skirt with **Right** sides together. Press seam open, then up toward the waistband. {fig. 9}

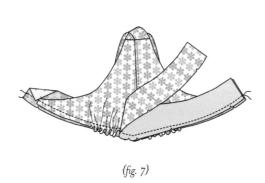

{fig. 7}

{fig. 8}

WAIST TIE VARIATION

1. Place 2 waist ties with **Right** sides together. Sew long edges and the one angled side, leaving center back open. Trim sewn corners, press seams open, and turn **Right** side out. Using a corner tool, gently push corners out. Press waist tie flat and topstitch ¼ in/6 mm from the 3 sewn edges.

2. With **Right** sides together, and raw edges aligned, place center back of completed waist tie and center back of interfaced waistband together; waist tie should be centered on waistband. Baste in place to hold the waist tie in position until invisible zipper is inserted. Repeat for second side. Make sure to only baste the ties to the interfaced waistband so that the zipper will be properly finished.

BUTTONHOLES FOR CROSS BACK STRAP VARIATION

1. Sew buttonholes (refer to pg. 138).

2. Sew buttons onto bodice after determining proper personal fit.

FINISHING

1. Press ⅝-in/1.6-cm seam allowance to **Wrong** side of raw edge of waistband facing.

2. Insert invisible zipper (refer to pg. 140) between top edge of interfaced waistband and notches on center back seam of skirt.

3. Working from the **Wrong** side of dress, enclose raw edges of waistband facing by stitching in the ditch (refer to pg. 142), topstitching, or hand sewing in place. {fig. 10}

4. Press ¼-in/6-mm hem allowance to **Wrong** side, then press up another ¼ in /6 mm, and topstitch.

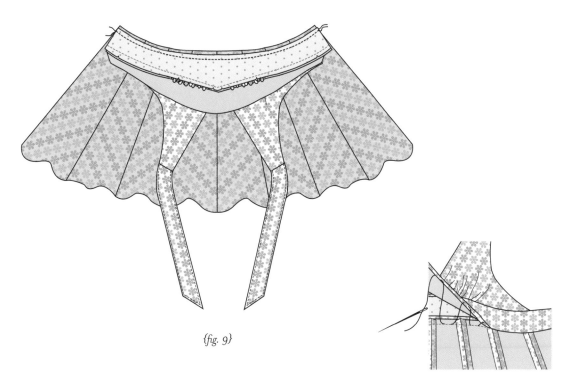

{fig. 9}

{fig. 10}

JACQUELINE KENNEDY ONASSIS

JACQUELINE KENNEDY ONASSIS

------ *Sewing Level: Beginner* ------

It is impossible to describe Jackie O. without using the word "classic." Her iconic style inspired minimalist fashionistas across the nation and continues to influence fashion trends today (Victoria Beckham, Katie Holmes, and Anne Hathaway are just a few current celebs who seek to embody the "Jackie" look). Though she first came into the public eye as the First Lady in 1961, Jackie's style had been developing for years, her fashion sensibility informed by an upbringing in an aristocratic New York family. Upon stepping into the spotlight, Jackie enlisted the designer Oleg Cassini to create a signature style for her, setting her apart from all previous First Ladies as a youthful, modern, and elegant role model for American women. She preferred A-line and shift dresses, simple pea coats with big buttons, pillbox hats, and white gloves, opting for minimal accessories (save her trademark pearls and big sunglasses). As she was a designer-conscious clotheshorse, it's only fitting that a Gucci handbag and sunglasses are named in her honor!

Both of these dresses exude the classic Jackie style with A-line skirt and wide necklines. The combination of the neck and waist darts gives the bodice a nice fitted shape while keeping seam lines clean and minimal.

The icon dress is more "First Lady" with the funnel neckline that sits up off the shoulders, framing the face elegantly.

The variation dress with the boat neckline is also a quintessential Jackie, perfect for jet-setting or lunching with the ladies. Add a practical touch to each dress option by sewing side seam pockets into the skirt. Everyone loves a dress with pockets!

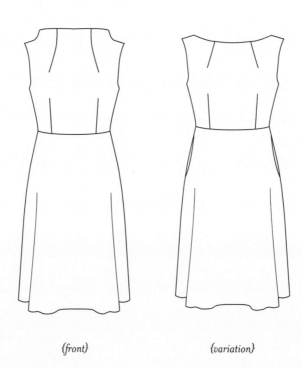

{front}   *{variation}*

{variation}

SUGGESTED FABRICS

Lightweight Wool, Stretch Poplin, Broadcloth, Linen, Denim, Twill

- - - YARDAGE - - -
2½ yds/2.3 m (45 in/115 cm wide)
- - - Or - - -
2 yds/1.8 m (60 in/150 cm wide)

- - - NOTIONS - - -
24-in/61-cm zipper
Thread to match

FOR BOAT NECK VARIATION:
Lightweight fusible knit interfacing: ½ yd/50 cm (44 in/112 cm wide) or 1 yd/90 cm (22 in/55 cm wide)

FOR FUNNEL NECK VARIATION:
Midweight fusible woven interfacing: ½ yd/50 cm (44 in/112 cm wide) or 1 yd/90 cm (22 in/55 cm wide)

FOLLOW CUTTING LAYOUT FOR PATTERN PIECES

1 Bodice Front (Variation)
2 Bodice Back (Variation)
3 Center Front Facing (Variation)
4 Side Front Facing (Variation)
5 Back Facing (Variation)
6 Skirt Front
7 Skirt Back
8 Pocket (optional)

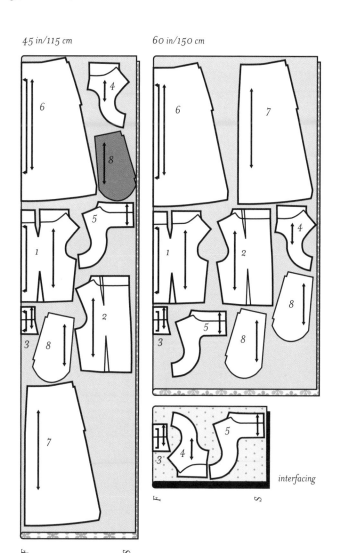

45 in/115 cm   60 in/150 cm

interfacing

SEWING INSTRUCTIONS

All seam allowances are ⅝ in/1.6 cm, unless otherwise indicated.

1. Cut out all pattern pieces from fabric, following cutting layout. Cut out interfacing for pattern pieces 3, 4, and 5.
2. Interface (refer to pg. 141) all facings.
3. Mark darts and circle markers with transfer paper, tailor's tacks, or an awl (refer to pg. 144).

PREPARE THE BODICE

1. Sew waist and neckline darts (refer to pg. 139) of front and back bodice pieces. Press dart bulk toward side seams.
2. With **Right** sides together, sew 1 side front facing to center front facing, aligning notches. Press seam open. Repeat for second side. {fig. 1}
3. With **Right** sides together, sew front bodice to 1 back bodice at shoulder seams only. For Funnel Neck Variation, reinforce the curve of the shoulder seam with a shorter stitch length, then clip (refer to pg. 139) to seam line. Press seam open. Repeat for second side and for front and back facings. {fig. 2}

ATTACH THE FACING

Tip: Trim seam allowances with a rotary cutter, using a cutting mat or a clean kitchen chopping block.

1. With **Right** sides together, sew facing to bodice along neckline and armholes, aligning seams and darts to notches. Trim, clip (refer to pg. 139), and press seams open. {fig. 3}
2. Turn bodice **Right** side out by pulling each back bodice through facings between neckline and armhole seams toward bodice front. Press facing to **Wrong** side of bodice at neckline and armhole.
3. With **Right** sides together, fold armhole facings up, align bodice front to bodice back and facing front to facing back at side seams. Sew from facing to waistline of bodice, aligning armhole seam lines. Press seams open, then press armhole facing to **Wrong** side of bodice. Repeat for second side. {fig. 4}
4. Stitch in the ditch (refer to pg. 142) of the side and shoulder seams to tack down facings.

Tip: Insert a wooden dowel or cardboard tube between facing and bodice at each shoulder to aid in pressing armhole and shoulder seams open.

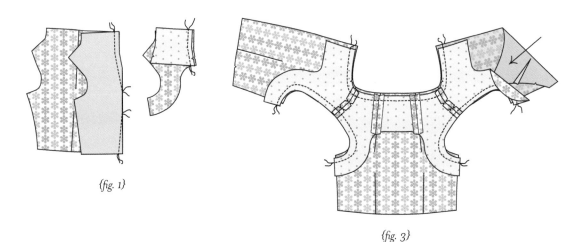

{fig. 1}

{fig. 3}

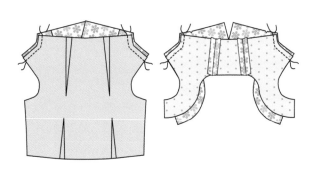

{fig. 2}

{fig. 4}

POCKETS

If side seam pockets are not desired, cut away ¼ in/6 mm where side seam on skirt front and back juts out. Sew skirt front to one skirt back with **Right** sides together. Press seam open. Repeat for second side and skip to next section.

1. Sew 1 pocket piece to skirt front at side seam where side seam juts out, using a ⅝-in/1.6-cm seam allowance. Press seam open, then toward pocket, and understitch (refer to pg. 143) seam allowance to pocket. Repeat for other side of skirt front and skirt backs. {fig. 5}

2. With **Right** sides together, place skirt front on 1 skirt back piece, aligning side seams, pockets and circle markers. Sew from waistline to top circle marker. Resume sewing at bottom circle marker to hemline. Press side seam open. Repeat for second side.

3. Sew around curve of pockets. Press pockets toward skirt front, aligning raw edges of waist and pocket tops and baste (refer to pg. 138) in place. {fig. 6}

ATTACH THE SKIRT

1. With **Right** sides together, sew bodice to skirt, aligning side seams and notches. {fig. 7}

FINISHING

1. Insert invisible zipper (refer to pg. 140) between the neckline and double notches on center back seam of skirt.

2. Press ¼-in/6-mm hem allowance to the **Wrong** side, then press up another 1¼ in/3 cm, and topstitch (refer to pg. 143) or hand sew.

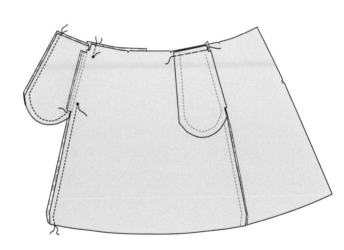

{fig. 6}

{fig. 5}

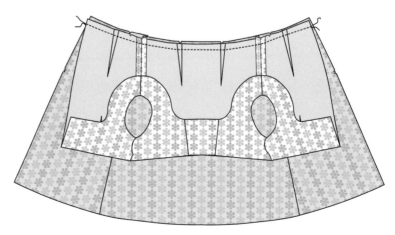

{fig. 7}

AUDREY HEPBURN

AUDREY HEPBURN

------ *Sewing Level: Beginner* ------

In a sea of curvy bombshells, Audrey Hepburn's sprightly looks and slight frame could have led to her getting swallowed up by the '50s Hollywood scene. Instead, she used her uniqueness to her advantage, creating an iconic look that still inspires imitation today. Hepburn chose elegant, clean lines that emphasized her slim physique, keeping her fashion choices simple and understated, much like fellow fashion star Jackie O. With her gentle demeanor and effortless style, Hepburn embodied a kind of timeless American glamour, exemplified by the Capri pants, ballet flats, and men's button-down shirts she wore off-screen. But she wasn't afraid to up the wow factor: the dress pictured here, a Givenchy evening gown of black Italian silk worn in *Breakfast at Tiffany's*, not only popularized the Little Black Dress as a fashion staple but also became so desired that in 2009 it was auctioned off at Christie's for close to $1 million.

Both of the Audrey dresses have a cowl drape along a boat neckline. The pencil skirt gathered at the waistline slims the waist and creates a more curved shape at the hips.

The icon dress is meant to be sewn as an LBD, but if black is not for you, we are sure Audrey would understand. The front bodice is cut on the bias, giving the cowl a nice drape. The back bodice has darts, providing more structure to the fit. Give the dress an evening look with Holly Golightly dazzle by adding feather to the hemline.

For a more casual interpretation, try cutting the variation from a knit fabric on the straight grainline. Still cute in black, although we know it is hard to resist all of those fabulous colored and printed knits out there. Pair it with a narrow belt and ballet flats, and we will still call you Audrey.

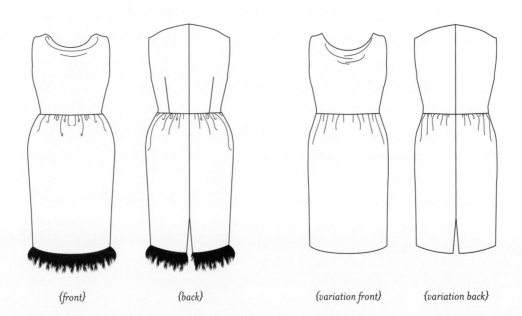

{front}   {back}   {variation front}   {variation back}

{variation}

SUGGESTED FABRICS

Satin, Lightweight Wool, Wool crepe, Brocade, Damask

- - - YARDAGE - - -

Not suitable for directional prints or stripes, nor for fabric without any bias give.

2⅞ yds/2.6 m (45 in/115 cm wide)

- - - Or - - -

2⅜ yds/2.2 m (60 in/150 cm wide)

- - - KNIT VARIATION - - -

Suitable for most 2-way midweight stretch knits

2⅜ yds/2.2 m (60 in/150 cm wide)

- - - NOTIONS - - -

24-in/61-cm invisible zipper (not needed for knit variation)

Thread to match

1⅓ yds/1.2 m feather or beaded trim, fringe, or other

Lightweight fusible knit interfacing: ½ yd/50 cm (45 in/115 cm wide)

FOLLOW CUTTING LAYOUT FOR PATTERN PIECES

1 Bodice Front (Variation) 3 Bodice Back Facing 5 Skirt Back

2 Bodice Back (Variation) 4 Skirt Front

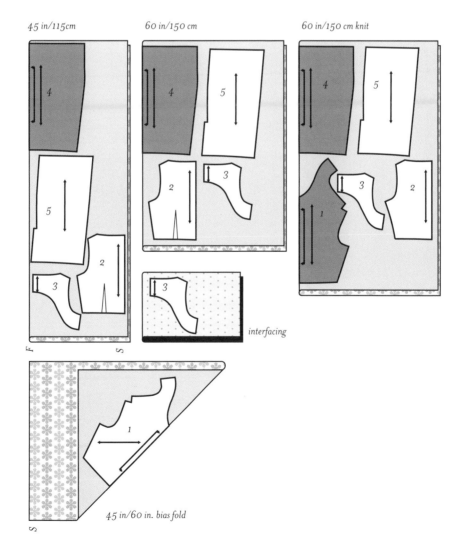

45 in/115cm   60 in/150 cm   60 in/150 cm knit

interfacing

45 in/60 in. bias fold

71

All seam allowances are ⅝ in/1.6 cm, unless otherwise indicated.

1. Cut out all pattern pieces from fabric, following cutting layout. Be aware of the variation markings on the bodice front and back pattern pieces for the knit variation. Cut out interfacing for pattern piece 3. If sewing with trim at hem, cut off ⅝ in/1.6 cm from skirt front and skirt back hem, noting that the hem of pattern pieces do not have any notches.

2. Interface (refer to pg. 141) back facing.

3. Mark darts and circle markers on bodice backs and skirt back with transfer paper, tailor's tacks, or an awl (refer to pg. 144). For the knit variation do not transfer markings or sew back bodice darts.

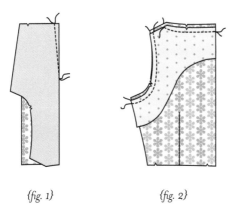

{fig. 1}   {fig. 2}

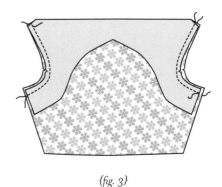

{fig. 3}

Knit Variation: Skip steps 1 and 3.

1. Sew darts (refer to pg. 139) on back bodice pieces. Press darts toward center back seam. *{fig. 1}*

2. With **Right** sides together, sew back facing to back bodice at armhole and neckline; leave shoulder seam open. Trim, clip (refer to pg. 139), and press seams open. Turn **Right** side out and press facing to **Wrong** side of bodice. Repeat for second side. *{fig. 2}*

3. Stay stitch (refer to pg. 142) around the entire bodice front.

4. With **Right** sides together, fold front bodice at fold line, aligning armhole notches. Sew armhole layers together, then trim, clip, and press seam open. Clip into the fold of the raw edge toward the staystitching at the shoulder. Repeat for second side. *{fig. 3}*

5. With **Right** sides together, place bodice back on bodice front. Slip the back bodice in between the fold of front. Align and sew the shoulder seams catching both bodices and facings. Turn **Right** side out. Press shoulder seam flat, then press front facing to **Wrong** side of bodice front. Repeat for second side. *{fig. 4}*

6. With **Right** sides together, fold armhole facings up, align bodice front to bodice back and facing front to facing back at side seams. Sew from facing to waistline of bodice, aligning armhole seam lines. Press seam open, then press facing at armhole to **Wrong** side of bodice. Repeat for second side. *{fig. 5}*

7. Stitch in the ditch (refer to pg. 142) of the side seams to tack down facings.

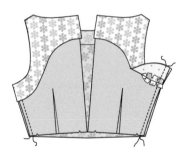

{fig. 5}

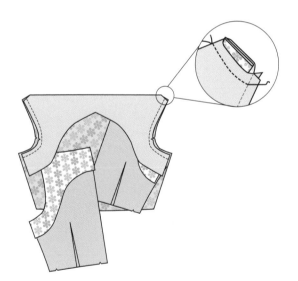

{fig. 4}

SKIRT

1. With **Right** sides together, sew skirt front to 1 skirt back at side seams, aligning notches. Press seam open. Repeat for second side. {fig. 6}

2. Sew 2 basting rows (refer to pg. 138) around waistline of skirt front and skirt backs between notches. Gather (refer to pg. 140) skirt waist, so that side seams and notches are aligned to the bodice. Make sure gathers are evenly spaced. {figs. 7, 8}

3. With **Right** sides together, sew bodice to gathered skirt, making sure side seams remain open. Remove basting stitches. {fig. 9}

Tip: Sew with **Wrong** side of bodice facing up, so that the gathering is against your feed dogs.

FINISHING

Knit Variation: Skip steps 1 and 2.

Instead place dress backs **Right** sides together, fold back facings up, align facing and waist seam lines, sew from facing to circle marker indicating the slit along the center back seam. Press seam open, then press facing back to **Wrong** side of bodice and stitch in the ditch to tack in position. Skip to step 3.

1. Insert invisible zipper (refer to pg. 140) between neckline and double notches on center back seam of skirt.

2. Cut 1 in/2.5 cm off the bottom corners of slit at a 45-degree angle to reduce bulk in the hem of slit and skirt.

3. Press ¼-in/6-mm seam allowance of slit to **Wrong** side, then press over another 1 in/2.5 cm.

For Trim Variation skip to next section.

4. Press ¼-in/6-mm hem allowance to **Wrong** side, then press up another 1 in/2.5 cm.

5 Finish hem of skirt and slit with desired hem finishing technique (refer to pg. 140).

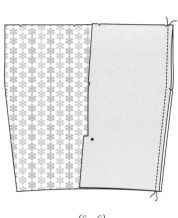

{fig. 6}

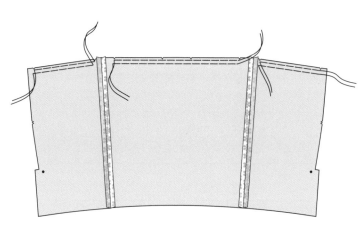

{fig. 7}

TRIM VARIATION

Sew trim with ⅝-in/1.6-cm seam allowance to hemline of skirt. Using a press cloth, press only the hemline of skirt to **Wrong** side, being careful not to scorch your trim. Hand sew hem tape in place to enclose seam allowances of hemline and trim.

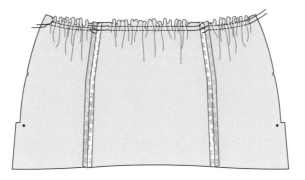

{fig. 8}

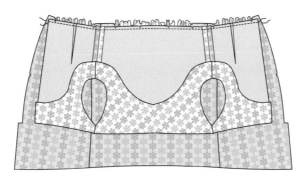

{fig. 9}

TWIGGY

TWIGGY

······ *Sewing Level: Intermediate* ······

Twiggy—still in her teen body and just seventeen years old when she broke onto the scene—seemed an unlikely successor to Marilyn Monroe, who had been the essence of style and beauty just a few years before. And yet, shortly after Monroe's death, Twiggy had taken the world by storm, being named the Face of '66 by the *Daily Express* and revolutionizing the fashion ideal with her mod, youthful style. With London's Swinging '60s as a backdrop, Twiggy carried the mod look, a combination of geometric prints and seam lines, high collars and higher hemlines, flirtatious buttons and bows, and baby doll dresses, all draped on her straight-as-an-arrow frame and topped off with an androgynous pixie haircut and mile-long fake lashes. America, still fully immersed in the British Invasion of rock, received Twiggy with open arms; she captured the youth, ambition, and self-image of the era. Twiggy achieved exactly the right balance of fun innocence and striking drama, her eyes alone seemed duplicitously coquettish and uncorrupt, an ambiguity underscored by her refusal to appear in revealing clothes. It was perhaps this modesty that led her to quit modeling after four years, though she is still credited with being the first modern supermodel, as well as pioneering perennially popular styles like the miniskirt.

It goes without saying that the Twiggy dress is a mini. Both dress options have a baby doll silhouette with oversized button plackets (pretty adorable, in our opinion). Seam lines at the bust and racer back armholes give the dress a more form fitting shape through the chest.

The icon dress has the mini hemline that Twiggy herself may have worn. Play up the geometry with large mod contrasting buttons and the fun circle pockets. For a more "Swinging London" look, sew the color block variation with the slightly longer hem length.

Each dress option can be sewn with either hemline and with or without pockets. They both look great over stockings, leggings, and—don't let Twiggy know we said so—skinny jeans.

{front}   *{variation}*

{variation}

SUGGESTED FABRICS

Lightweight Linen, Broadcloth, Cotton Batiste, Crepe, Double Knit

- - - YARDAGE - - -
3 yds/2.75 m (45 in/115 cm wide)
- - - Or - - -
2¼ yds/2 m (60 in/150 cm wide)

- - - YARDAGE FOR COLOR BLOCK VARIATION - - -
For Self: 1½ yds/1.4 m (45 in/115 cm or 60 in/150 cm wide)
For Skirt Contrast 2: 1 yd/1 m (45 in/115 cm or 60 in/150 cm wide)
For Bodice Contrast 3: ½ yd/46 cm (45 in/115 cm or 60 in/150 cm wide)
For Placket/Neckband Contrast 4: ½ yd/46 cm (45 in/115 cm or 60 in/150 cm wide)

- - - NOTIONS - - -
Four 1-in/2.5-cm buttons
Thread to match
Contrast Pearl cotton thread or embroidery floss (for variation)
Lightweight fusible knit interfacing: ⅞ yd/80 cm (44 in/112 cm wide) or 1¾ yd/1.6 m (22 in/55 cm wide)

FOLLOW CUTTING LAYOUT FOR PATTERN PIECES

1 Bodice Front	5 Placket	9 Pocket (optional)
2 Bodice Back	6 Front Armhole Facing	10 Pocket Interfacing
3 Skirt Front	7 Back Armhole Facing	(optional)
4 Skirt Back	8 Neck Band	

45 in/ 115cm

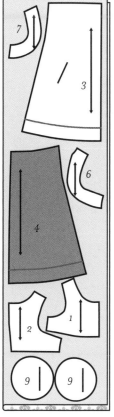

60 in/150 cm

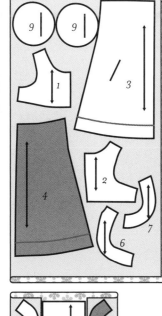
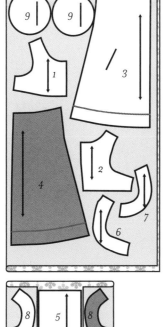
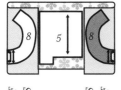

45/60 in Color Block

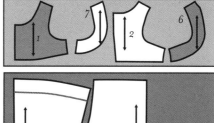
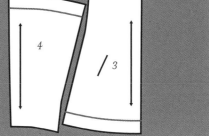

All seam allowances are ⅝ in/1.6 cm, unless otherwise indicated.

1. Cut out all pattern pieces from fabric, following cutting layout. Cut out interfacing for pattern pieces 5, 6, 7, 8, and, if pockets are desired, 10.

2. Interface (refer to pg. 141) button placket, one neck band, two front armhole facing pieces (one right and one left) and two back armhole facing pieces (one right and one left). For circle Pocket Variation, interface **Wrong** side of skirt front according to pocket placement guidelines.

3. Mark all stitch lines, fold lines, circle markers, button and buttonhole placement with transfer paper, tailor's tacks, or an awl (refer to pg. 144).

1. With **Right** sides together, sew bodice front to skirt front, aligning notches. Press seam open. Repeat for second side, making sure to have a right and left dress front. For color block variation, sew self bodice to contrast skirt. For second side, sew contrast bodice to self skirt. {fig. 1}

2. With **Right** sides together, sew bodice back to skirt back, aligning notches. Press seam open. Repeat for second side, making sure to have a right and left dress back. For color block variation, sew self bodice to contrast skirt. For second side, sew contrast bodice to self skirt. {fig. 2}

3. With **Right** sides together, sew center front bodices, aligning seam lines; make sure bodice seams remain open. Press center front seam open. {fig. 3}

4. With **Right** sides together, sew center back bodices, aligning notches and seam lines; make sure bodice seams remain open. Press seam open.

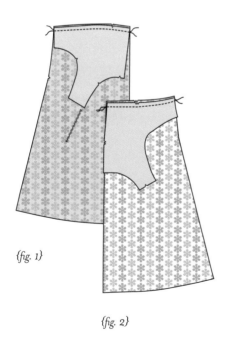

{fig. 1}

{fig. 2}

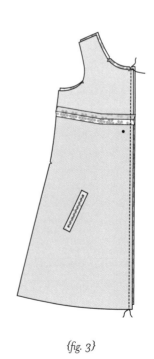

{fig. 3}

1. Place placket on dress front with both **Wrong** sides facing up, aligning circle markers.

2. Sew along marked stitch line. Reinforce the corners of the stitch line with a shorter stitch length. {fig. 4}

3. Cut both layers open along the marked cut line, making sure to not cut past the stitch line. {fig. 5}

4. Fold button side of placket toward **Right** side of dress front. {fig. 6} Edge stitch (refer to pg. 139) both sides of the button placket. Be sure to fold under and enclose raw edges as you topstitch (refer to pg. 143). {fig. 7}

5. Fold buttonhole side of placket toward the **Right** side of dress front. The bottom seam allowance of the button side of the placket will be pushed toward the **Right** side of dress front. {fig. 8}

6. Edge stitch both sides of the buttonhole placket without stitching on top of button placket. {fig. 9} Stack the buttonhole placket on top of the button placket. Press seam allowances under and trim if necessary. Sew around all 4 sides of the base of the buttonhole placket, catching the dress front and the seam allowances of the button placket, enclosing all raw edges. {fig. 10}

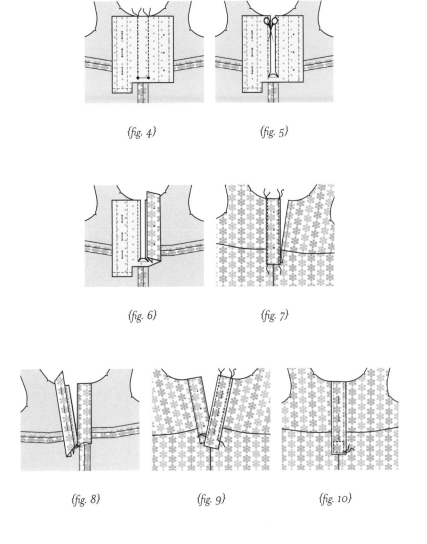

{fig. 4}　　　　{fig. 5}

{fig. 6}　　　　{fig. 7}

{fig. 8}　　　{fig. 9}　　　{fig. 10}

POCKET VARIATION

Tip: If you want to hand sew a decorative running stitch out of pearl cotton thread or embroidery floss, do so using your machine stitches as a guide to get even hand-sewn stitches around the circle pocket and its opening.

1. With **Right** sides together, place one pocket piece on dress front, aligning marked stitch lines. Sew these pieces together with a short stitch length along markings. *{fig. 11}*

2. Cut along marked cut lines, up to stitch line. Press each side of pocket toward the opening. *{fig. 12}*

3. Push pocket through opening toward the **Wrong** side of dress front. Press pocket opening flat so that seams are along fold. Topstitch ¼ in/6 mm around pocket opening. *{fig. 13}*

4. With **Right** sides together, place a second pocket piece, over the first pocket piece, on **Wrong** side of dress front. With **Wrong** side facing up, sew around pocket edges, through all layers. *{fig. 14}*

Repeat steps 1 through 4 for second pocket.

Tip: Use a lot of pins and mark a circular sewing line with tailor's chalk. This will create a beautifully sewn circle on the dress front.

ARMHOLE FACING

1. With **Right** sides together, sew dress front to dress back at shoulder seam only. Press seam open. Repeat for second side.

2. Sew front armhole facing to back armhole facing at shoulder seam. Press seam open. Repeat for second side.

3. With **Right** sides together, sew armhole facing to armhole of dress. Trim, clip (refer to pg. 139), and press seam open. Press seam allowance toward facing and under-stitch (refer to pg. 143). *{fig. 15}*

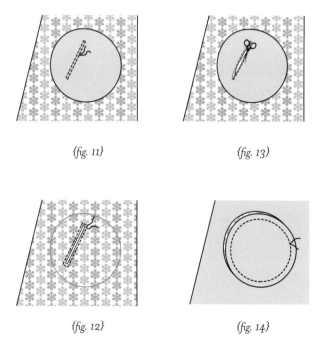

{fig. 11}

{fig. 13}

{fig. 12}

{fig. 14}

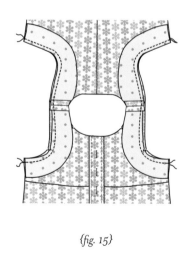

{fig. 15}

ATTACH THE NECKBAND

1. Stay stitch (refer to pg. 142) the neckline of the dress. Clip every inch or so to release the seam allowance around the curves.

2. Sew interfaced neckband to dress at neckline, catching the armhole facing where the seam allowances overlap. Make sure that your seam hides the staystitching, so that it does not show on the outside of your finished dress. Trim, clip, and press seam allowance toward neckband. {fig. 16}

3. Place neckbands **Right** sides together, aligning top edge and side where they meet the placket, ensuring circle markers on the neckbands are aligned. Sew the neckband from the circle marker, pivoting at corners, continuing around neckline, and ending at the opposite marker. Trim and clip seam allowances. Press the neckband piece that isn't interfaced toward **Wrong** side of dress. {fig. 17}

4. Press the seam allowance of the inside neckband edge under. On the **Right** side of the garment stitch in the ditch (refer to pg. 142), or topstitch to enclose raw edges of the inside neckband.

SIDE SEAMS

1. With **Right** sides together, fold armhole facings up, align dress front to dress back and facing front to facing back at side seams. Sew from facing to hemline, aligning at armhole seam lines, bodice seam lines and notches. Press seam open, then press facing at armhole to **Wrong** side of bodice. Repeat for second side.

2. Stitch in the ditch on side seams to tack the armhole facings in place.

FINISHING

1. Sew buttonholes (refer to pg. 138) on placket and neckband. Sew buttons in place.

2. Press ¼-in/6-mm hem allowance to the **Wrong** side, then press up another 1 in/2.5 cm, and topstitch or hand sew.

{fig. 16}

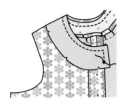

{fig. 17}

DIANA ROSS

DIANA ROSS

------ Sewing Level: Beginner ------

It's difficult to stand out, style-wise, in an era of billowing bell-bottoms and shimmering disco balls, but Diana Ross was up to the task. Combining the sequins, rhinestones, and sparkle of the emerging disco culture with the polished American sportswear that was at its height in the '70s, Ross created a distinct look that rivaled her famous pipes for awe-inspiring impact. Her look evolved with her career, beginning with a flippy bob and baby-doll dresses during the Supremes era, then moving on to a bold Afro and wide-cut trousers as she embarked on her solo career. She settled on the style for which she's most known after starring in *Mahogany*, a film–fittingly–about an aspiring fashion designer, for which Ross is credited with costume design. The daring diva's ultimate look consisted of striking sleeved jersey gowns, pussycat blouses, and fabulous accessories, topped off by a full mane of natural curls along with heavy eyeliner and false lashes (two big trends of the era, perhaps inspired by Ross's contemporary, Twiggy). Never safe and always sexy, Ross brought bling to the music world and is credited as being one of the first female African American pop culture icons.

Diana opens her arms when she opens those pipes, so there is no better place to add drama to this dress than the sleeves. Incorporate some disco details with your choice of 3 keyhole openings on the center front seam: modest (above bust), revealing (below bust), and sexy (to the navel), or no keyhole at all. Both dresses are slim though the waist and hips, to keep the focus up top. This dress sews up the quickest of any in the book, so if you need to make a dramatic impression in a hurry, go with Diana.

The icon dress has wide dolman sleeves that flutter around relaxed arms but are bold like butterfly wings when you are belting out the lyrics to "I'm Coming Out" with outstretched arms.

The variation takes that dramatic sleeve and gathers it into a long cuff that starts at the elbow. If this feels too covered-up for you and not quite disco enough, add slits to the sleeves from the shoulder to the elbow.

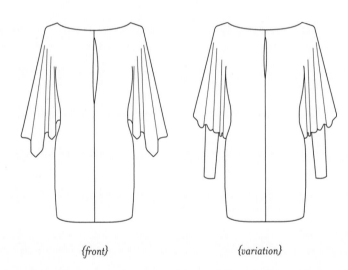

{front}   {variation}

{variation}

SUGGESTED FABRICS

Suitable for most 2- or 4-way stretch knit fabrics. Not suitable for rib knits.

- - - **YARDAGE** - - -

2½ yds/2.3 m (60 in/150 cm wide)

- - - **NOTIONS** - - -

Thread to match

Lightweight fusible knit interfacing: sufficient for front facing

FOLLOW CUTTING LAYOUT FOR PATTERN PIECES

1 Dress Front and Back   2 Keyhole Facing   3 Cuff (Variation)

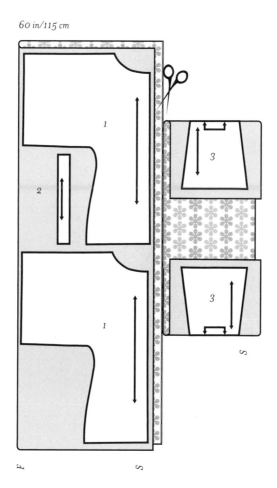

60 in/115 cm

95

SEWING INSTRUCTIONS

All seam allowances are ⅝ in/1.6 cm, unless otherwise indicated. Use a stretch stitch (refer to pg. 143) on your machine for all seams unless otherwise indicated.

1. Cut out all pattern pieces from fabric, following cutting layout. Note that the fabric is folded along length grain just wide enough to fit the dress front and back pattern pieces. Cut off excess fabric, ensuring the cuff pattern piece fits. Fold the excess fabric top down and the bottom up along the cross grain. Place cuff patterns on each fold. Cut out interfacing for pattern piece 2.

2. Interface (refer to pg. 141) keyhole facing.

ATTACH THE FACING

If you do not want a keyhole, skip this step. Note: The illustrations exhibit construction of a "sexy" keyhole.

1. With **Right** sides together, using a straight stitch, sew keyhole facing to dress front from notch at neckline to notch at desired depth of keyhole. Press seam open, then press seam allowance toward facing. Understitch (refer to pg. 143) with a straight stitch through facing and seam allowances. Repeat for second side. {fig. 1}

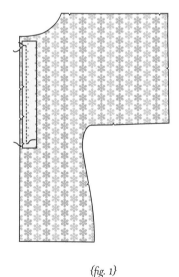

{fig. 1}

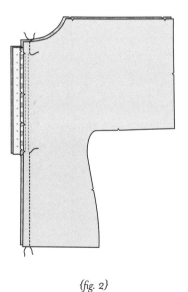

{fig. 2}

DRESS

1. With **Right** sides together, sew center front of dress from neckline to notch at top of facing. Resume sewing from notch at bottom of facing and sew to hemline of dress. For a dress without a keyhole, sew from neckline to hem. Press seams open. Stitch in the ditch (refer to pg. 142) at the center front seam to tack facing down. *{fig. 2}*

2. With **Right** sides together, sew center back seam of dress from neckline to hemline. Press seam open.

3. With **Right** sides together, sew dress front to dress back at shoulder seam. Press seams open.

If the sleeve slit is desired, sew from neckline to notch, resume sewing from notch to hem of sleeve. Around slit, press seam allowance to wrong side and topstitch ¼ in/6 mm from edge. Repeat for second side. *{fig. 3}*

4. With **Right** sides together, sew dress front to dress back at side seams. Clip seam allowance of armhole curve. Press seam open. Repeat for second side. *{fig. 4}*

NECKLINE

1. Stay stitch (refer to pg. 142) neckline at ⅝-in/ 1.6-cm seam allowance. Trim seam allowance to ¼ in/6 mm. Press seam allowance to **Wrong** side and topstitch (refer to pg. 143) with a twin needle (refer to pg. 143), catching the keyhole facing.

Tip: When using a twin needle, always sew with the garment **Right** side facing up. Make sure to loosen the thread tension on your machine.

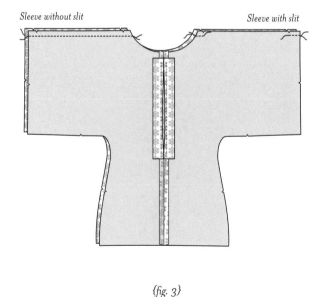

Sleeve without slit   *Sleeve with slit*

{fig. 3}

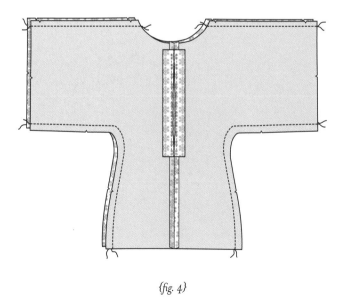

{fig. 4}

If not doing the cuff variation, skip ahead to the Finishing section.

1. With **Right** sides together, fold cuff along length grain, aligning notches. Sew down the long edge. *{fig. 5}*

2. Turn half **Right** side out so that the sleeve cuff will be self-lined with seam allowances hidden. *{fig. 6}*

3. Sew 2 basting (refer to pg. 138) rows around hem of sleeve and gather (refer to pg. 140) sleeve in order to fit to the raw edge cuff opening. *{fig. 7}*

4. Turn dress **Wrong** side out, place cuff inside sleeve with **Right** sides together, align cuff seam with dress side seam, notches and raw edges. *{fig. 8}* Make sure gathers are evenly spaced and pin well! Sew sleeve to cuff. Remove basting stitches. Repeat for second side. *{fig. 9}*

Tip: Sew from the inside of the cuff, so that the gathering is against your feed dogs. Additionally, sewing with the cuff side up will allow you to sew the circular seam more easily without having to stretch the seam around the arm of your sewing machine.

{fig. 5}

{fig. 6}

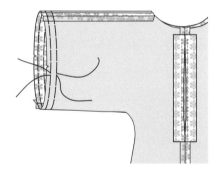

{fig. 7}

1. Press ⅝-in/1.6-cm hem allowance to **Wrong** side around base of dress. Topstitch using the twin needle.

2. Press ⅝-in/1.6-cm hem allowance to **Wrong** side around base of sleeve. Topstitch using the twin needle. Skip this step for the cuff variation (cuffs are self finished because they're folded).

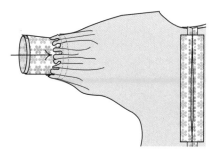

{fig. 8}

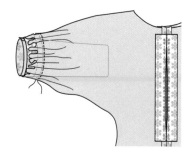

{fig. 9}

FARRAH FAWCETT

FARRAH FAWCETT

------ *Sewing Level: Beginner/Intermediate* ------

For most people, Farrah Fawcett calls to mind one thing: the hair. Feathered, flouncy, fabulously blown-out hair. And in many ways, this is fitting, since the undeniable energy of her legendary locks exemplified the carefree athleticism and joy that made Fawcett's personality such a welcome counterpoint to the withdrawn waifs of the late '60s and early '70s. In addition to her wholesome image as a healthy, tanned, all-American girl, Fawcett also embraced her inherent sexuality, infamously eschewing bras and marketing her image in the infamous red bathing suit pin-up poster. "When [Charlie's Angels] was number three, I figured it was our acting—when it got to be number one, I decided it could only be because none of us wears a bra," Fawcett once said, exhibiting both her self-aware sexuality and approachable humor. Her playful-yet-suggestive style came through in choices like high-waisted denim flares, jumpsuits, track jackets, and, as pictured here, the wrap dress, likely inspired by none other than Diane von Furstenberg, the must-have dress of the decade.

This wrap dress says casual grace and sexiness. The deep V-neck dress can be worn in the Charlie's Angels style showing more cleavage, or more demure and sweet with a camisole underneath.

The icon dress is a working girl interpretation of the wrap with more professional details: three-quarter length sleeves with tabs, a collar, and a mini pocket. After all, detective work requires looking sharp.

The variation is a streamlined, carefree, capped sleeve wrap, perfect for picnicking in the park.

Mix and match the elements of each variation and without a doubt you will capture the classic Farrah and liberated '70s style.

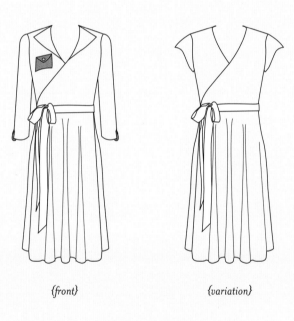

{front}   {variation}

{variation}

SUGGESTED FABRICS

Suitable for most light- to midweight 2-way stretch fabrics. Not suitable for rib knits.

- - - YARDAGE - - -
2½ yds/2.3 m (60 in/150 cm wide)
Lightweight cotton sufficient for pockets and tabs

- - - NOTIONS - - -
Two or three ½-in/12-mm buttons (optional for pocket and tab variations)
1-in/2.5-cm grosgrain ribbon: 3¾ yds/3.4 m
Thread to match
Lightweight fusible knit interfacing: ¾ yd/69 m (22 in/55 cm wide)

FOLLOW CUTTING LAYOUT FOR PATTERN PIECES

1 Bodice Front
2 Bodice Back
3 Short Sleeve (optional)
4 Three-Quarter Sleeve (optional)

5 Skirt Front
6 Skirt Back
7 Front Neck Facing
8 Back Neck Facing

9 Collar (optional)
10 Skirt Facing
11 Tab (optional)
12 Pocket (optional)

SEWING INSTRUCTIONS

All seam allowances are ⅝ in/1.6 cm, unless otherwise indicated. Use a stretch stitch (refer to pg. 143) on your machine for all seams unless otherwise indicated.

1. Cut out selected pattern pieces from fabric, following the cutting layout. Cut out interfacing for pieces 7, 8, 9 (optional), and 10.

2. Interface (refer to pg. 141) facings, 2 tabs, and 2 collar pieces (making sure to have a left and a right collar).

3. Cut grosgrain ribbon in half crosswise.

PREPARE COLLAR (OPTIONAL)

1. With **Right** sides together, sew interfaced collar to noninterfaced collar; leave long, slightly curved side open. Trim, clip (refer to pg. 139), and press seam open, then turn **Right** side out. Using a corner tool (refer to pg. 144) gently push out corner and press flat. Repeat for second side. {fig. 1}

2. Topstitch (refer to pg. 143) around the sewn edges on both collars, ¼ in/6 mm from the edge.

ATTACH THE FACING

1. With **Right** sides together, sew bodice front to bodice back at shoulder seams. Press seam open. Repeat for second side. {fig. 2}

2. Sew front facing to back facing at shoulder seams with **Right** sides together. Press seam open. Repeat for second side. {fig. 3}

3. Baste (refer to pg. 138) the open edge of collar between shoulder seam and notch located along neckline of bodice front with **Right** sides facing up. Repeat for second side.

4. Baste one cut edge of grosgrain ribbon to **Right** side of bodice front on the short edge between the neckline and waistline. Repeat for second side.

5. Sew facing to bodice with **Right** sides together along neckline, pivoting at the corners and sandwiching the collar and grosgrain ribbon. Trim, clip (refer to pg. 139), and press seam open. {fig. 4}

6. Press seam allowances toward the facing and understitch (refer to pg. 143).

{fig. 1}

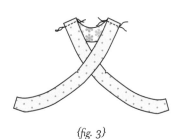

{fig. 3}

{fig. 2}

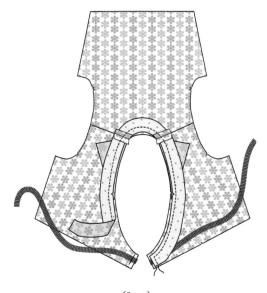

{fig. 4}

PREPARE THE BODICE

1. Place bodice front to bodice back with **Right** sides together.
2. For left side of bodice as worn, sew side seam. Press seam open.
3. For right side as worn, sew side seam from the waistline up ⅝ in/1.6 cm toward the armhole. Leave a 1 in/2.5 cm opening for the grosgrain ribbon. Sew remainder of side seam toward the armhole. Press seam open. *{fig. 5}*

SLEEVES

1 With **Right** sides together, fold short sleeve, and sew from underarm to sleeve hem. Press seam open. Repeat for all sleeve pieces. For Three-Quarter Sleeve Variation, skip to step 3.
2. For Cap Sleeve Variation: With **Right** sides together, sew sleeve and sleeve self lining along hemline, making sure to create a right and left sleeve. Trim and clip seam allowance, turn **Right** side out and press flat. Baste sleeve to sleeve self lining at armhole to prevent shifting. *{fig. 6}*
3. With **Right** sides together, place top of sleeve opening to armhole of bodice, aligning raw edges, notches, underarm seam lines, and the shoulder seam to the notch at the top of the sleeve.
4. With **Wrong** side of the bodice facing up, sew from the underarm seam lines around armhole, stretching the fabric slightly to align notches and smooth out any creases or puckers as you sew. Trim, clip, and press seam allowances toward **Wrong** side of bodice. Repeat for second side. *{fig. 7}*

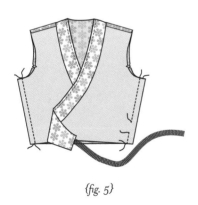

{fig. 5}

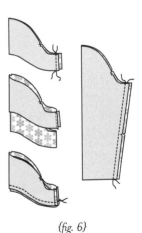

{fig. 6}

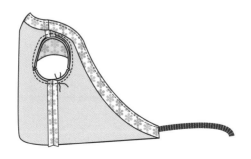

{fig. 7}

PREPARE THE SKIRT

1. With **Right** sides together, sew skirt facing to skirt front, pivoting at bottom hem to create a nice clean corner. Trim corner and turn **Right** side out. Press seam open, then press toward facing and understitch. Repeat for second side, making sure to have a right and left skirt front. {fig. 8}

2. Sew skirt front, opposite skirt facing, to skirt back at side seam, aligning notches. Press seam open. Repeat for second side. {fig. 9}

3. Unfold the front facings; with **Right** sides together, sew skirt to bodice, ensuring all seam lines are aligned and seams remain open. {fig. 10}

4. Fold facing back toward **Wrong** side. Stitch in the ditch (refer to pg. 142) at both front waistlines and each shoulder seam to tack facing toward **Wrong** side. Alternatively, you could topstitch (refer to pg. 143) the facings in position.

POCKET (OPTIONAL)

1. With **Right** sides together, sew pocket pieces, starting along the bottom edge and pivoting (refer to pg. 142) at all corners. Make sure to leave a 1-in/2.5-cm opening at bottom of pocket, to turn it **Right** side out.

2. Trim all corners, turn **Right** side out, and gently push out all corners using a corner tool (refer to pg. 144). Press the seam allowances of the opening to the **Wrong** side of the pocket. Press triangular flap toward outside of pocket square. Hand tack or sew a button through all layers of the pocket to secure the triangle flap in position.

3. Try dress on and mark desired pocket placement. Lay bodice flat and pin pocket in position. Edge stitch (refer to pg. 139) around sides and bottom of pocket, leaving top flap edge open.

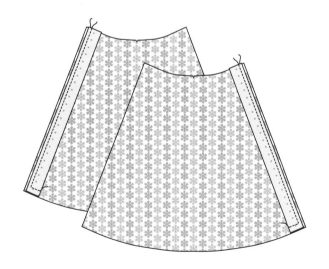

{fig. 8}

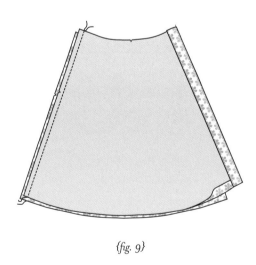

{fig. 9}

FINISHING

1. Try dress on, mark your desired hemline with a yardstick measuring up from the floor. Use tailor's chalk or pins to mark a cut or fold line. Shorten as desired.

2. Press ⅝-in/1.6-cm hem allowance to **Wrong** side around base of dress and three-quarter sleeve (if using). Topstitch using a twin needle (refer to pg. 143).

Tip: When using a twin needle, always sew with the garment **Right** side facing up. Make sure to lower the thread tension on your machine.

TAB (OPTIONAL)

1. With **Right** sides together, sew tab with a ¼-in/6-mm seam allowance, pivoting at all corners; leave short straight side open. Trim corners, press seams open, and turn **Right** side out.

2. Using a corner tool, gently push out any corners. Topstitch around with a ¼-in/6-mm seam allowance.

3. Try on three-quarter sleeve and mark desired placement of tab. For a slightly scrunched sleeve, pin unsewn end of tab to **Wrong** side of sleeve, then pull triangular end to the **Right** side and mark position.

4. Align unsewn edge of the tab with the hem allowance on the **Wrong** side of the sleeve. Sew directly on top of the sleeve hemline. Bring triangular end of tab to the **Right** side of sleeve to the marking. Hand tack or sew a button through all layers of tab and sleeve to secure in position.

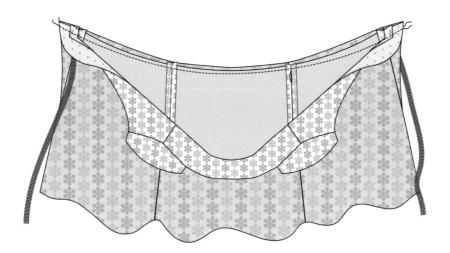

{fig. 10}

STEVIE NICKS

STEVIE NICKS

------ *Sewing Level: Beginner* ------

When Stevie Nicks first began her music career in the early '70s, she sported clothes scoured from secondhand stores. Before long, she was making enough money to snap up all the designer duds she wanted, though she stayed true to her glam-gypsy look, an aesthetic that resonated with the hippie culture of the era. These humble roots may explain why everyday folk emulate her look, even though designers haven't snapped her up as the face of their labels. "Fashion people have always talked about me like 'that's a very Stevie Nicks maxi-coat' or 'that's a very Stevie Nicks chiffon skirt,'" she says, "but nobody really came to me." Despite this sentiment, Nicks has had a major impact on fashion, and her style likely influenced alt-divas like Madonna. Nicks, in turn, says she drew inspiration for her look from the feathers, bell-bottoms, and silky blouses of Janis Joplin. Her signature look has been refined over the years, but long skirts, lacy shawls, leather, lots of layers, untamed hair, and her famous suede 7-inch platform heels have been a constant throughout a four-decade career.

This dress would not say "Stevie" without a handkerchief hemline. Both of these dress options feature a simple fitted bodice, so as not to overpower the beautiful lace or chiffon shawl you will most likely drape over your shoulders.

The icon dress uses fold over elastic to create matching or contrasting spaghetti straps. For a more free-spirited look, add fringe along the neckline. We like the way the fringe drapes nicely over the bust, giving it nice movement as you rock out to "Dreams."

The variation has a gathered cap sleeve instead of the spaghetti straps and the neckline is finished off with facings. This interpretation is a nod to Stevie's more evolved look, Victorian meets gypsy ballerina.

{front}   {variation}

{variation}

SUGGESTED FABRICS

Suitable for most lightweight 2- or 4-way stretch fabrics. Not suitable for rib knits.

--- **YARDAGE** ---
2⅜ yds/2.2 m (60 in/150 cm wide)

--- **NOTIONS** ---
Thread to match
¼-in/6-mm elastic for cap sleeve: 1½ yds/1.4 m
Fold over elastic for spaghetti strap variation: 2 yds/1.8 m
Lightweight fusible knit interfacing: sufficient for front and back facing
Optional Fringe for front and back neckline: ¾ yd/69 cm

FOLLOW CUTTING LAYOUT FOR PATTERN PIECES

1 Bodice Front
2 Bodice Back
3 Front Facing
   (Cap Sleeve Variation)
4 Back Facing
   (Cap Sleeve Variation)

5 Skirt (extend pattern pieces
   10 in/ 25 cm from selected size)
6 Sleeve (Cap Sleeve Variation)
Fold Over Elastic Guide for Armhole
   (Spaghetti Strap Variation)

Elastic Guide for Sleeve Armhole
   (Cap Sleeve Variation)
Elastic Guide for Sleeve Shoulder
   (Cap Sleeve Variation)

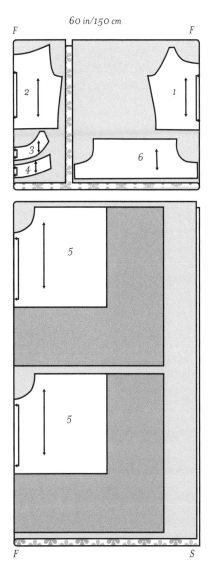

60 in/150 cm

SEWING INSTRUCTIONS

All seam allowances are ⅝ in/1.6 cm, unless otherwise indicated. Use a stretch stitch (refer to pg. 143) on your machine for all seams unless otherwise indicated.

1. When tracing skirt pattern piece 5, extend 10 in/25 cm on the 2 sides indicated on pattern piece. {fig. 1}

2. Cut out all pattern pieces from fabric, following cutting layout. For Cap Sleeve Variation, cut out interfacing for pieces 3 and 4 and elastic using armhole and shoulder guidelines. For the Spaghetti Strap Variation, refer to fold over elastic guideline for armhole.

3. Interface (refer to pg. 141) facings.

BODICE WITH FOLD OVER ELASTIC AND OPTIONAL FRINGE

For Cap Sleeve Variation skip to next section.

1. Cut ⅜ in/1 cm off front and back bodice neckline seam allowance.

2. Cut fold over elastic pieces to fit to neckline of front and back bodices.

3. With fold over elastic open, place on bodice front with **Wrong** sides facing. Make sure the crease in the fold over elastic is directly above the neckline edge. Sew elastic to bodice with a wide zigzag stitch with **Right** side of bodice facing up. Repeat for back bodice. {fig. 2}

4. Cut fringe to fit neckline of front and back bodices and baste (refer to pg. 138) to **Right** side of bodice.

5. Fold elastic to **Right** side of front bodice enclosing neckline edge and fringe. Sew across with a zigzag stitch. Remove basting stitches from **Wrong** side of bodice. Repeat for back bodice.

6. With elastic open, flat, and **Right** sides together, fold one armhole elastic, making sure that it is not twisted, and sew the short ends together, making a continuous circle. Repeat for second side.

7. With **Right** sides together, sew front bodice to back bodice at side seams. Press seam open. Repeat for second side. {fig. 3}

8. Align fold over elastic seam with side seam of bodice and place with **Wrong** sides facing. Pin in position along armhole. Using a zigzag stitch, begin sewing at back bodice neckline and stopping at the front bodice neckline. {fig. 4}

9. Fold elastic along crease line, encasing the bodice armhole and creating a spaghetti strap. With a zigzag stitch, sew all the way around the armhole. {fig. 5}

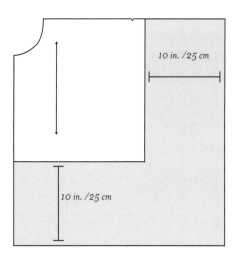

{fig. 1}

{fig. 2}

1. With **Right** sides together, sew front facing to front bodice along neckline. Trim, clip (refer to pg. 139), and press seam open. Repeat for back bodice. {fig. 6}

2. Press seam allowance toward facing and understitch (refer to pg. 143). Repeat for back bodice.

3. With **Right** sides together, sew bodice front to bodice back at side seams. Press seams open. {fig. 3}

{fig. 3}

{fig. 4}

{fig. 5}

{fig. 6}

1. Press top edge of sleeve down ¼ in/6 mm, then press down another ⅜ in/1 cm. Topstitch along folded edge creating a casing. Repeat for second sleeve and for sleeve bottoms.

2. Using a safety pin, feed the armhole elastic through sleeve casing. Once the opposite end of elastic has reached the opening of casing, secure in place. Push the safety pin to open end of casing, gathering fabric as you go. Make sure the elastic is not twisted and secure elastic at each opening. Repeat for all sleeve casings. *{fig. 7}*

3. Sew sleeve underarms together, catching the elastic in the seam. Stay stitch elastic in place along shoulder seams. *{fig. 8}*

4. Place sleeve and bodice armholes, **Right** sides together, aligning all notches and side seam lines. Fold facings down over the top of sleeves so that **Right** side of facing is on **Wrong** side of sleeve. Sew armhole. Repeat for second side. *{fig. 9}*

5. Trim and clip (refer to pg. 139) seam allowance. Fold facings to **Wrong** side of bodice. Topstitch along front neckline, ⅜ in/1 cm from edge. Repeat at back neckline.

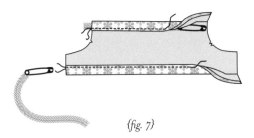

{fig. 7}

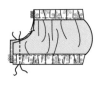

{fig. 8}

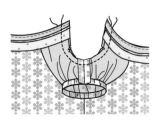

{fig. 9}

1. With **Right** sides together, sew skirt side seams, aligning notches. Press seam open. Repeat for second side. {fig. 10}

2. With **Right** sides together, sew skirt to bodice, making sure side seams are aligned and remain open. {fig. 11}

Choose between two hemline finishes: a rolled hem (refer to pg. 140) by machine or serger or a double fold hem by pressing hemline up ¼ in/6mm, then press up another ¼ in/6 mm, and topstitch.

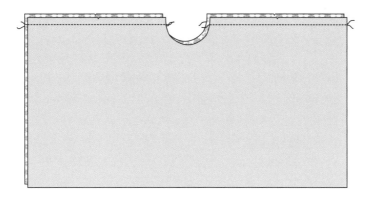

{fig. 10}

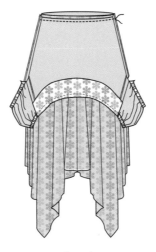

{fig. 11}

MADONNA

MADONNA

To say that Madonna has one iconic look would be to contradict her very essence, which stems from her constant image reinvention. Still, the outfit pictured here—a corset-topped wedding dress with lace gloves, piles of pearls, chains, and crucifixes, plus a "Boy Toy" belt to hammer home the tongue-in-cheek shock value—perfectly embodies the Madonna persona that took the nation by storm in the mid-eighties. Madonna didn't consider herself beautiful, and so she sought sex appeal through a different route, by pushing boundaries and provoking conservatives. (A self-professed "fallen Catholic," she saw spirituality and sexuality as inextricably linked, offending many with her risqué religious fashion choices.) With her captivating visage, in-your-face personality, and über-sexy style, Madonna changed the shape of fashion in the '80s and '90s, immediately sparking a line of Madonna-wear ("sportswear for sexpots," she called it), and inspiring teenage girls to re-create the Madonna look (known at the time as "flash-trash") with undergarments worn over skirts, cheap and gaudy jewelry, loose T-shirts, lace and lingerie, and a serious dose of attitude.

Corset seam lines were the starting point for this design and, as with Madonna, this dress can take on endless renditions.
Have fun and mix and match all of the options.

The icon dress has a "Like a Virgin" lace overlay on the bodice. Add layers and layers of tulle under the skirt to build volume.
If you cannot find a vintage "Boy Toy" belt, wide elastic with a nice clasp will work just as well.

The "Vogue" variation is created by stitching charmeuse to the knit foundation before cutting out a pattern inspired by none other than
the cone-busted corset designed by Jean Paul Gaultier. Sew the knit or silk skirt to the bodice.

If **Desperately Seeking Susan** is more your aesthetic, skip the silk and lace and opt for an all-knit variation, but please:
accessorize, accessorize, accessorize!

{front}   {variation}

{variation}

SUGGESTED FABRICS

4-way Stretch knit combined with either stretch lace or charmuese. Tulle for petticoat.

- - - YARDAGE - - -
Knit: 1⅜ yds/1.3 m (60 in/150 cm wide)
Stretch Lace Variation: Stretch Lace: 1 yd/90 cm (45 in/115 cm wide)
Tulle: 1⅜ yds/1.3 m (60 in/150 cm wide)
Silk Cutwork Variation: Charmeuse: ½ yd/50 cm (45 in/155 cm wide)

- - - NOTIONS - - -
Thread to match
⅝-in/1.6-cm wide trim for accenting bodice seam lines and creating straps: 1¾ yds/1.6 m (optional)

FOLLOW CUTTING LAYOUT FOR PATTERN PIECES

1 Center Front Bodice   4 Center Back Bodice   6 Strap
2 Side Front Bodice   5 Side Back Bodice   7 Skirt
3 Bust

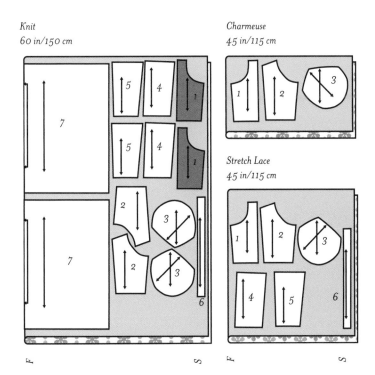

All seam allowances are ⅝ in/1.6 cm, unless otherwise indicated. Use a stretch stitch (refer to pg. 143) on your machine for all seams unless otherwise indicated.

1. Cut out all pattern pieces from fabric, following the cutting layout. Be aware of the grainline variation on the bust pattern piece for the Silk Cutwork Variation.

2. Mark all circle markers with transfer paper, tailor's tacks, or an awl (refer to pg. 144).

Silk Cutwork Variation and Stretch Lace Variation

1. For the Silk Cutwork and Lace Overlay Variations, baste (refer to pg. 138) contrast fabric (stretch lace or charmeuse) to knit fabric with **Right** sides up around the perimeter of all bodice pieces: side front and back, center front and back, and bust. For the Silk Cutwork Variation this only applies to front bodice pieces: side, center, and bust. *{fig. 1}*

2. Trace off all stitch and cut lines onto **Wrong** side of fabric.

3. For Silk Cutwork Variation, using a zigzag stitch, sew along marked stitch lines with **Wrong** sides facing up.

4. Carefully cut only the charmeuse along the marked cut lines. Be sure to use sharp fabric scissors and take nice steady strokes so that a clean cut is made. Take out basting stitches to make it easier to cut. *{fig. 2}*

1. Separate your bodice pieces, one set for the outermost bodice of the dress and one set for the lining. You should have 2 of each bodice piece in each stack. Steps 2 through 6 are referring to the outer pieces. Repeat steps 2 through 6 for the bodice lining.

2. With **Right** sides together, sew center front bodice to side front bodice, aligning notches. Press seam open. Repeat for second side. *{fig. 3}*

3. With **Right** sides together, sew center front bodices. Press seam open. For Silk Cutwork Variation, align stitch and cut lines of the charmeuse when sewing bodices together. *{fig. 4}*

4. With **Right** sides together, sew center back bodice to side back bodice. Press seam open. Repeat for second side. *{fig. 5}*

5. With **Right** sides together, sew center back bodices, aligning notches. Press seam open. Repeat for second side. *{fig. 6}*

If using eyelet tape or any other decorative trim along the bodice seam lines, topstitch in place, ensuring that no metal accents are in the seam allowances.

6. With **Right** sides together, sew bodice front to bodice back at side seams. Press seam open. Repeat for second side. *{fig. 7}*

7. Repeat steps 2 through 6 for bodice self lining.

{fig. 1}

{fig. 2}

{fig. 3}

{fig. 4}

{fig. 5}

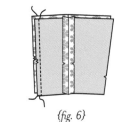

{fig. 6}

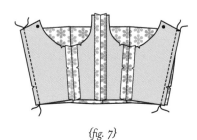

{fig. 7}

If using eyelet tape or other trim for the strap, use strap pattern piece to determine proper length and skip step 1.

1. With **Right** sides together, fold strap in half along the length grain. Sew long side with ¼-in/6-mm seam allowance. Turn **Right** side out. Repeat for second strap. *{fig. 8}*

Tip: Use a loop turner (refer to pg. 144) or safety pin for ease in turning the straps **Right** side out.

2. Stay stitch strap to bust at the top center-most notch, aligning raw edges. Repeat for second side. *{fig. 9}*

3. With **Right** sides together, sew each bust self lining to bust (with or without contrast) between the notches located on each side of the strap. Trim, clip (refer to pg. 139), and press seam open. Turn **Right** side out and topstitch along sewn edge with a zigzag or stretch stitch. Repeat for second side. *{fig. 10}*

4. Sew 2 rows of basting stitches (refer to pg. 138) between bottom 2 notches of bust. Repeat for second side. *{fig. 11}*

5. Gather (refer to pg. 140) the bust and align to notches on front bodice. Repeat for second side. *{fig. 12}*

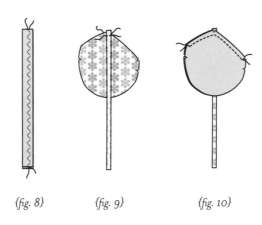

{fig. 8}   {fig. 9}   {fig. 10}

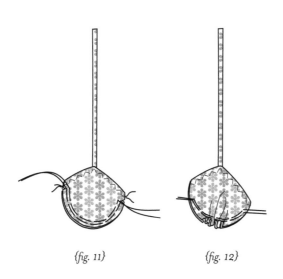

{fig. 11}   {fig. 12}

1. With **Right** sides together, place outer bust to outer front bodice, aligning finished edges of bust to circle markers on front bodice and notches. Ensure gathers are evenly spaced. Sew together carefully as these are opposing curves. Remove basting stitches. Repeat for second bust. {*fig. 13*}

2. With **Right** sides together, making sure strap is not twisted, place along seam line of center and side back bodices, aligning raw edges. Stay stitch (refer to pg. 142) in position. Try on partially assembled bodice, adjust fit as necessary.

3. With **Right** sides together, place bodice self lining to bodice front, aligning top edges; bust pieces will be sandwiched between the self lining and outer bodice. Starting at one side seam, sew carefully around the busts, pivoting at the circle markers and continuing around entire bodice top, until your stitches overlap. With **Wrong** side of outer bodice facing up, use previous stitch lines around the bust as guidelines. Trim and clip seam allowances. Turn **Right** side out and press flat. {*fig. 14*}

Tip: Pin the straps away from the seam line so that they do not accidentally get sewn into your neckline.

{*fig. 13*}

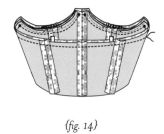

{*fig. 14*}

1. With **Right** sides together, sew side seams of skirt. Press seams open. Repeat for second side. For Tulle Variation, repeat for multiple layers until you have your desired fullness. {*fig. 15*}

2. Sew 2 basting rows along top of skirt. Gather to align side seams and notches to seam lines on bodices. If using the tulle, sew 2 basting rows to both skirt and tulle together, with **Right** sides facing up. {*fig. 16*}

3. With **Right** sides together, using a zigzag stitch, sew skirt to bodice. Remove basting stitches. {*fig. 17*}

1. Tulle edges can be left raw.

2. Press hemline up ⅝ in/1.6 cm and topstitch using a twin needle (refer to pg. 143).

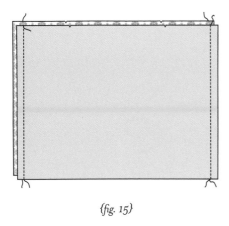

{*fig. 15*}

{*fig. 16*}

{*fig. 17*}

TERMS, TECHNIQUES, AND TOOLS

Backstitching: Backstitching is used at the beginning and end of every seam, to lock stitches in place. Sew 3 to 5 stitches forward then 3 to 5 stitches backward, then forward again; continue to the end of the seam and repeat. This will prevent the seams from unraveling.

Baste: A long stitch length sewn by hand or machine without backstitching. Basting stitches are used as marking guides, for gathering, or to temporarily hold a seam together. They can be easily removed after seams are finished.

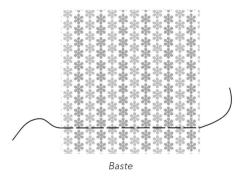

Baste

Bias grainline: When a fabric is cut from a pattern piece that utilizes a bias grainline, it is cut so that the natural cross and length grains are at a 45-degree angle. This allows for the greatest stretch in the fabric and it accentuates the curves of the body with a beautiful drape. When working with bias-cut fabrics it's important to stay stitch around the perimeter of the cut fabric to prevent the fabric from becoming distorted. When preparing to sew, pin often and carefully. To avoid seams that are wavy, be sure not to pull or stretch the fabric when sewing; just let the machine pull the fabric under the presser foot.

Buttonholes: Refer to your sewing machine manual for specific instructions on how to set up your machine to properly sew a buttonhole. Always make sure that the fabric is stabilized with interfacing and that the fabric is **Right** side up when sewing. Once the buttonhole is sewn, apply a little fray check to the **Right** and **Wrong** sides of your fabric to prevent the fabrics from fraying where you cut your buttonhole open. To open the buttonhole, carefully cut with thread-cutting scissors. Start in the middle and cut toward each end, being careful not to cut past the stitches. Always test sew a buttonhole on an interfaced scrap of your final fabric, to make sure the tension is set properly for your fabric and thread, and to check the fit of the button.

Casing: Fabric tube used to enclose elastic or drawstring, created by folding fabric and leaving an opening for access.

Circle markers: These are the small circles located on the pattern pieces. They indicate critical alignment of cut fabric pattern pieces, such as pockets, plackets, or godets. They also indicate pivot points on a corner and can be used to indicate placement for other surface details.

Clip: In order for a neckline or armhole to lay flat, it is necessary to first trim the seam allowance and then, at a right angle from the raw edge of the seam, cut to just short of the stitching line, allowing the seam to spread.

Clip

Darts: Transfer all dart markings onto **Wrong** side of fabric using transfer paper or tailor's tacks. Start sewing at the widest opening of the dart and sew toward the point. As you approach the point, reduce the stitch length on your machine and finish by sewing off the edge of the fabric without backstitching. Cut thread tails long enough to double knot them.

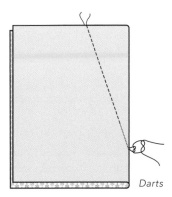

Darts

Edge stitch: Generally used with a straight stitch to hold layers of fabric together and help seams lay flat. Edge stitching is often used on pockets and usually refers to sewing ⅛ in/3 mm or less from the finished edge or seam.

Gather: Sew two parallel rows of basting stitches; one within the seam allowance at ½ in/12 mm and the other at ¾ in/2 cm from the raw edge. Holding the two bobbin threads (one from each row), gently pull the threads, creating small folds in the fabric. In most instances, sewing two rows is preferable to sewing one, as the gathers are stabilized. Once the gathered seam is sewn, remove basting stitches carefully with your seam ripper.

Hem finishing: There are several methods of hem finishing; here are just a few examples.
1. Rolled hem: Creates a narrow hem, appropriate for many delicate and lightweight fabrics. Refer to your sewing machine manual for instructions on how to attach the rolled hem foot, then attach the foot to your sewing machine. On the piece to be hemmed, press ⅛ in/3 mm, then another ⅛ in/3 mm to the **Wrong** side of the fabric, for the first 2 in/5 cm to be hemmed. Place the pressed edge under the foot, hold the thread tails back, and begin sewing.
2. Single fold: Press up hem allowance and topstitch. This hem does not encase the raw edges, so it's best to treat the raw edge with desired seam finishing technique. This is great for knits, especially when using a twin needle.
3. Double fold: Press hem allowance up twice and topstitch.
4. Rolled hem with serger: Refer to your serger manual for specific instructions on how to set your machine up properly. Prepare your fabric, making sure hemline is trimmed to desired length without seam allowance and raw edges are neatly trimmed. The threads on a rolled hem wrap tightly around the fabric, creating a delicate but secure finish.

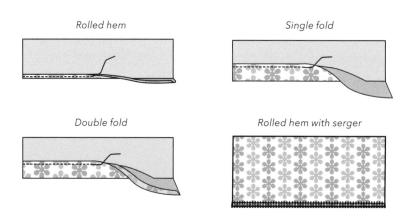

Rolled hem

Single fold

Double fold

Rolled hem with serger

Inserting an invisible zipper:
1. Interface the **Wrong** side of the seam allowance for the length of the zipper to be inserted. Use a strip of lightweight fusible knit interfacing 1¼ in/3.2 cm wide. {fig. 1}
2. Prepare your zipper by pressing the teeth flat, using a low heat setting on your iron.
3. Using a chalk wheel or fabric marker, draw ⅛ in/3 mm from the raw edge between neck and double notches on center back seam of the garment.
4. With **Right** sides together, place open zipper on garment. Align the top teeth of the zipper with the center back seam line where it meets the facing and the edge of the zipper tape to the line drawn in step 3. Machine or hand baste zipper in place. {fig. 2}

5. Using the invisible zipper foot and adjusting your needle position dependent on the instructions relevant to your machine, sew as close to the zipper teeth as possible without sewing on the zipper teeth. Sew from the top of the zipper toward the bottom, getting as close as you can to the zipper pull while maintaining proper distance from zipper teeth and seam allowance.
6. Repeat steps 4 and 5 for second side. Ensure that your seam lines align across your zipper and that your zipper is not twisted. {fig. 3}
7. Close zipper and sew from double notches on center back seam to hemline or circle marker indicating a slit opening, overlapping zipper seam lines slightly. {fig. 4}
8. Fold neck facing **Right** sides together on dress aligning raw edges of fabric to the zipper tape. Sew within the seam allowance the length of the facing. Turn **Right** side out, forcing the facing back to the **Wrong** side of dress. {fig. 5}

Inserting a zipper

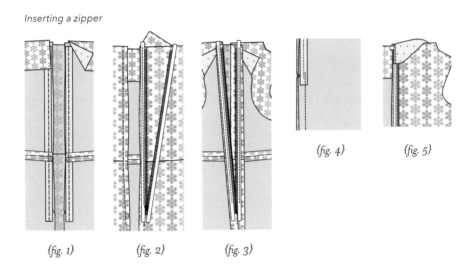

{fig. 1}   {fig. 2}   {fig. 3}   {fig. 4}   {fig. 5}

Interface: Before interfacing, make sure your fabric is pressed flat. Protect your ironing board by covering it with some scrap fabric. Place the interfacing scratchy (glue) side up on your ironing board and lay your fabric on top of it, with the **Wrong** side down. Using a press cloth and an iron setting appropriate for your fabric, place the iron down for a count of ten, holding it in place; lift and move the iron so that you overlap the previously fused section and continue in this manner until all the fabric is fused to the interfacing. Let fabric cool before handling, so that the adhesive can set.

Interfacing: Used to stabilize or add structure to certain areas of the garment. Lightweight fusible knit interfacing is used throughout the book. Follow the instructions to determine which pattern pieces need to be interfaced.

Interlining: A layer of fabric, commonly flannel, cotton batiste, or silk organza, sewn between the outer and lining fabrics to give additional strength and support. Interlining is also helpful when working with sheer fabrics.

Notches: The triangle shapes that are along the perimeter of the pattern pieces and extend ¼ in/6 mm into the pattern. When cutting out your fabric, clip in just to the depth of the triangle; remember to clip in twice when there are two notches side by side. Never cut any deeper than the triangle, as it will result in a hole along your seam line. Notches are used to align pattern pieces along seam lines.

Pivot: Sew toward the corner and stop before the edge, maintaining the seam allowance. Lower the needle into the fabric, lift the presser foot, and rotate the fabric toward you. If the newly rotated edge is aligned to the seam allowance guideline, lower the presser foot and continue sewing. If not, take additional stitches using the hand crank, *not* the foot pedal. A visual cue for when to pivot the fabric is when the edge of the fabric is approaching, but not past the front edge of the presser foot.

Right side/Wrong side: The **Right** side or face of the fabric is the side you want showing on the outside of your garment. The **Wrong** side refers to the inside or side that faces the body.

Seam allowance: The distance between the raw edge of your cut fabric and the seam line that will be created by thread as you sew. Always measure from your needle position to the right side of your presser foot to ensure proper seam allowance. Use masking tape or a magnetic seam guide to mark the distance accurately.

Seam finishing: There are several methods of finishing. Here are just a few examples.
1. Serger/overlock: Trims any excess thread or fabric, as it creates an overlock stitch around the raw edges of the fabric. Be careful not to cut beyond your seam allowance.
2. Pinking: Specialized pinking shears cut the fabric in a zigzag shape in order to minimize fraying.
3. Zigzag/overcast: To achieve the best look, use an overcasting foot in conjunction with a zigzag or overlock stitch to finish off the raw edges of the fabric. Refer to your sewing machine manual for instructions specific to your machine.

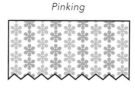

Serger/overlock   *Pinking*   *Zigzag/overcast*

Stay stitch: Stitching line just within the seam allowance used to keep certain areas of the garment from getting stretched or distorted while handling. This is generally done to just one thickness of fabric. Stay stitching is particularly useful on necklines, armholes, curved seams, and fabric cut on the bias.

Stitch in the ditch: Keeps the facing or lining from rolling to the **Right** side of the garment. With the **Right** side facing up, topstitch through the facing and fabric, right in the seam so that it becomes hardly visible. Be sure to use thread that matches your fabric or a shade darker for best results.

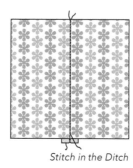

Stitch in the Ditch

Stretch stitch: If using a sewing machine (and not a serger) to sew up a knit garment, it's important to utilize the stretch stitch on your machine so that your seams will stretch with your fabric. This stitch gives the appearance of a straight stitch but is slightly stretchy. There are generally three options on most modern sewing machines: the simple zigzag, generally set to a stitch length and width setting of 2–3; the straight stretch stitch, which looks like a triple stitched row; and the multi-stitch zigzag, which is a series of small stitches in the zigzag pattern (see diagram). If you are new to working with knits, we suggest sewing with the simple zigzag stitch, as it is the easiest to seam rip.

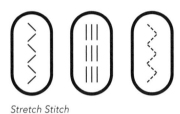

Stretch Stitch

Topstitch: Generally used with a straight stitch to hold layers together and help seams lay flat. It usually refers to sewing ¼ in/6 mm from the finished edge or seam.

Trim: In order for a neckline or armhole to lie flat and to reduce bulk, it is necessary to cut the seam allowance to ¼ in/6 mm and is often combined with clipping. Trimming also refers to diagonally cutting away almost all the seam allowance of a sewn corner to reduce fabric bulk when turned **Right** side out.

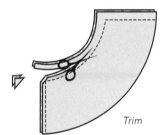

Trim

Twin needle: Creates two parallel stitching lines, often around the hemline of a sleeve or skirt. This works great with knits. Sew with your fabric **Right** side facing up. Make sure to lower the thread tension on your sewing machine. Be sure to test on a scrap of your fabric to check the tension and stretch. Refer to your sewing machine manual for setup and threading instructions.

Understitch: Press the seam allowance toward the facing or lining. Working with the fabric **Right** side up, topstitch through the facing or lining and seam allowances as close to the seam as possible. Understitching helps to keep facings and linings toward the inside of your garment.

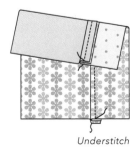

Understitch

Awl: Sharp tool used to make small holes in fabric to indicate where circle markers are on your pattern paper. *{fig. 1}*

Corner tool: A blunt stick that is used to help define corners by pushing the fabric bulk out of an interior corner or dart points. NEVER use your scissors to do the job of a corner tool. *{fig. 2}*

Loop turner: Used to pull tubular narrow pattern pieces, such as straps, **Right** side out. *{fig. 3}*

Press cloth: Used to protect your iron and fabric from heat distortion and interfacing's adhesives—lightweight woven cotton, or silk organza work well. *{fig. 4}*

Ruler: Our favorite ruler to have in the sewing room is the clear 2-in by 18-in, gridded ruler. It makes it easy to check seam allowances and trace patterns. *{fig. 5}*

Tailor's tacks: Thread temporarily hand sewn to your fabric to mark pattern information (darts, circle markers, button placement, etc.). Great to use when transfer paper or awl punches are not appropriate for fabric. Transfer information from paper pattern to fabric by taking one stitch with a hand sewing needle and thread, leaving tails about 1 in/2.5 cm long and unknotted so that they do not fall out but are easy to separate from paper pattern and to remove from fabric when sewing is complete.

Transfer paper: When used with a tracing wheel, it transfers stitching lines, fold lines, and other placement guidelines onto the wrong side of your fabric. Sometimes referred to as tracing paper or dressmaker's carbon, it is commonly made of a waxy or chalky lined paper, similar to carbon paper. Always test on your fabric and make sure it washes away, so you're not left with a permanent mark on your fabric. *{fig. 6}*

Tracing wheel: Leaves perforated marking on paper if tracing off a pattern. Also used with transfer paper to transfer markings from the paper pattern to the **Wrong** side of fashion fabric for plackets, darts, pockets, and more. *{fig. 7}*

{fig. 1}

{fig. 2}

{fig. 3}

{fig. 4}

{fig. 5}

{fig. 6}

{fig. 7}

RESOURCES

B BLACK AND SONS
A wool wonderland in the heart of LA's garment district, plus great tailoring supplies
548 South Los Angeles Street
Los Angeles, CA 90013
(213) 624-9451/ (800) 433-1546
www.bblackandsons.com

B&J FABRICS
525 7th Avenue
New York, NY 10018
(212) 354-8150
www.bandjfabrics.com

BOLT
2136 NE Alberta Street
Portland, OR 97211
(503) 287-bolt
www.boltfabricboutique.com

BRITEX FABRICS
Our hometown dream has an amazing selection of fashion fabrics, trims, and notions.
146 Geary Street
San Francisco, CA 94108
(415) 392-2910
www.britexfabrics.com

BROOKLYN GENERAL STORE
128 Union Street
Brooklyn, NY 11231
(718) 237-7753
www.brooklyngeneral.com

CLOTILDE
Great sewing notions and tools
(800) 545-4002
www.clotilde.com

CRAFTY PLANET
2833 Johnson Street NE
Minneapolis MN 55418
(612) 788-1180

DENVER FABRICS
www.denverfabrics.com

DISCOUNT FABRICS
201 11th Street
San Francisco, CA 94103
415.495-4201
www.discountfabrics-sf.com

DPI
Print your own fabric
645 Mariposa Street
San Francisco, CA 94107
415 407-1919
www.dpi-sf.com

eBAY
With a little digging, you can find great vintage fabrics by the yard.
www.ebay.com

ETSY
Everything from vintage yardage to trims from several sellers
www.etsy.com

FABRIC OUTLET
2109 Mission Street
San Francisco, CA 94110
(415) 552-4525

FISHMAN'S FABRICS
1101 South Desplaines Street
Chicago, IL 60607
(312) 922-7250
www.fishmansfabrics.com

FLEA MARKETS
Great source for vintage fabrics, fashions and accessories
Research events in your area.

GAIL K. FABRICS, INC.
2216 Cheshire Bridge Road NE
Atlanta, GA 30324
(404) 982-0366
www.gailkfabricsinc.com

GOLDEN D'OR FABRIC OUTLET
Harry Hines Boulevard
Dallas, TX 75220
(214) 351-2339

GOLDEN SILKS
www.goldensilks.net

HANCOCK FABRICS
1600 Saratoga Avenue, sp505
San Jose, CA 95129
(408) 871-0145
www.hancockfabrics.com

IKEA
Yes, they have everything including fabric by the yard
www.ikea.com

JOANN'S
(888) 739-4120
www.joann.com

KNITTN KITTEN
Vintage fabrics and notions
7530 N.E. Glisan Street
Portland, OR 97213
(503) 255-3022
www.knittnkitten.com

M&J TRIMMING
Fringe and feathers among thousands of other trimmings
1008 Sixth Avenue
New York, NY 10018
(212) 391-6200
www.mjtrim.com

MICHAEL LEVINE'S
A favorite treasure in the heart of LA's garment district
920 Maple Avenue
Los Angeles, CA 90015
(213) 622-6259
www.mlfabric.com

MILL END STORE
9701 SE McLoughlin Boulevard
Portland, OR 97222
(503) 786-1234
www.millendstore.com

MILL END TEXTILES
Multiple Midwest locations
http://millendtextiles.com/

MOOD LOS ANGELES
6151 W. Pico Boulevard
Los Angeles, CA 90035
(323) 653-6663

MOOD NEW YORK
225 W 37th Street, 3rd Floor
New York, NY 10018
(212) 730-5003
www.moodfabrics.com

MYSTERY MISTER
1506 Haight Street
San Francisco, CA 94117
www.mysterymister.com

PEAPOD FABRIC
1314 18th Avenue
San Francisco, CA 94122
(415) 731-3206
www.peapodfabrics.com

PENDLETON WOOLEN MILLS: WOOLEN MILL STORE
8550 Southeast McLoughlin Boulevard
Portland, OR 97222
(503) 535-5786

PURL PATCHWORK
147 Sullivan Street
New York, NY 10012
(212) 420-8798
www.purlsoho.com

REPRO DEPOT
www.reprodepotfabrics.com

SATIN MOON
32 Clement Street
San Francisco, CA 94118
(415) 668-1623

THE SEWING PLACE
Great interfacing selection and sewing notions
(775) 853-2207
www.thesewingplace.com

SEW, MAMA, SEW!
(503) 380-3584
www.sewmamasew.com

SEWZANNE'S FABRICS
Large selection of fold over elastic and knits that are targeted at kids
www.sewzannesfabrics.com

SPOONFLOWER
Print fabric of your own design or shop the printed fabrics that other artists have designed.
www.spoonflower.com

SR HARRIS
8865 Zealand Avenue N.
Brooklyn Park, MN 55445
(763) 424-3500
www.srharrisfabric.com

STONE MOUNTAIN AND DAUGHTER
518 Shattuck Avenue
Berkeley, CA 94704
(510) 845-6106

THAI SILKS
52 State Street
Los Altos, California 94022
(800) 722-7455/ (650) 948-8611
www.thaisilks.com

THRIFT STORES
Many a good treasure can be found at your local thrift store for vintage yardage, fashions and accessories. Explore your area for hidden treasures.

TREADLE YARD GOODS
1338 Grand Avenue
St. Paul, MN 55105
(651) 698-9690

URBAN BURP
Rare vintage and reproduction fabrics
70 Columbus Avenue
San Francisco, CA 94133
(415) 399-8761
www.urbanburp.com

VOGUE FABRICS
623–627 W. Roosevelt Road
Chicago, IL 60607
(312) 829-2505
www.voguefabricsstore.com

ZIPPERSTOP/A. FEIBUSCH CORP.
27 Allen Street
New York, NY 10002
(888) 947-7872 / (212) 226-3964
www.zipperstop.com

ZUCKER FEATHER PRODUCTS
(573) 796-2183/ (800) 346-0657
www.zuckerfeather.com

BLOGS

FAMOUS FROCKS
*Yes. that's right, a blog dedicated to this book. We
would love to see your interpretations of these dresses.*
www.famousfrocks.com

A DRESS A DAY
www.dressaday.com

ALICIA PAULSEN
www.rosylittlethings.typepad.com/posie_gets_cozy

ANGRY CHICKEN
www.angrychicken.typepad.com/angry_chicken

ANNA MARIE HORNER
www.annamariahorner.blogspot.com

BLOESEM
www.bloesem.blogs.com

BURDA STYLE
www.burdastyle.com

COLETTE PATTERNS
www.colettepatterns.com/blog

DESIGNSPONGE
www.designspongeonline.com

GERTIES NEW BLOG FOR BETTER SEWING
www.blogforbettersewing.com

LENA CORWIN
http://blog.lenacorwin.com

PATTERN REVIEW
www.sewing.patternreview.com

PRINT AND PATTERN
www.printpattern.blogspot.com

PURL BEE
www.purlbee.com

THE SARTORIALIST
www.thesartorialist.blogspot.com

SEW MAMA SEW
www.sewmamasew.com/blog2

SOULEMAMA
www.soulemama.com

UNIFORM STUDIO
www.uniformnatural.com/blog

REFERENCE BOOKS

READER'S DIGEST COMPLETE GUIDE TO SEWING

THE SEWING BOOK BY ALLISON SMITH

ACKNOWLEDGMENTS

There are countless people to whom we are grateful for their support, encouragement, and inspiration. We both would like to thank all of our sew testers who gave us not only great feedback but encouragement too: Allison Page, Anna Toth, Bryna McLane, Chloe Sinclair, Claire Fong, Crystal Herman, Heidi Alexander, and Liz Lavoie Capron.

We also want to thank the entire posse that worked on creating an amazingly fun photo shoot for our Web site, www.chroniclebooks.com/famousfrocks. Raul Anthony and Krysti Lozinsky made all of our fabulous models not only look the part but feel it too. To our models, you were more than we ever hoped and dreamed—thank you, Nancy Deane, Laura Lee Mattingly, Michelle Clair, and Ayako Akazawa. To our photographer, Daniel Castro and Marc and Scott, the crew, you were true gentlemen, and your warmth and vision brought out our most playful selves. To Jenna Cushner, thank you for bringing all of the dresses to life through your superb styling.

Thank you, Laura Lee Mattingly, our editor, for inviting us to work on this amazing project and making us look good while doing it.

------ *Sara* ------

I want to thank my husband, Stephan, for his unwavering support and countless hours coaching me through the illustrations. And to my son, Nasen, thanks for being able to recognize the difference between a funnel and boat neckline.

------ *Hannah* ------

I would like to thank my partner, Francois, for his unconditional love and support throughout this process. Thank you to my parents, Mark and Elizabeth, for encouraging all of my creative endeavors, and to my sisters and best friends, Melodie and Rachel.